# RECLAIMING THE HUMANITIES

## The Roots of Self-Knowledge in the Greek and Biblical Worlds

# R. Thomas Simone
# Richard I. Sugarman

UNIVERSITY
PRESS OF
AMERICA

LANHAM • NEW YORK • LONDON

Copyright © 1986 by
R. Thomas Simone and Richard I. Sugarman

University Press of America,® Inc

4720 Boston Way
Lanham, MD 20706

3 Henrietta Street
London WC2E 8LU England

Printed in the United States of America

**Library of Congress Cataloging in Publication Data**

Simone, R. Thomas (Reno Thomas), 1943-
   Reclaiming the humanities.

   Includes index.
   1. Greece—Civilization—To 146 B.C.   2. Humanities.
3. Civilization, Occidental—Greek influences.   4. Bible
—Influence—Civilization, Occidental.   I. Sugarman,
Richard Ira.   II. Title.
DF78.S58   1986       938       85-22605
ISBN 0-8191-5093-2 (alk. paper)
ISBN 0-8191-5094-0 (pbk. : alk. paper)

# Acknowledgments

We would like to thank the many people who have helped in the preparation of this book. We are particularly grateful to our colleague, Robert J. Anderson, for his lucid contribution on purpose and happiness in Aristotle. In addition to his essay, he has given us much advice and encouragement in the writing of this work.

For assistance in typing, proofreading, and indexing we would like to thank, Heather Casavoy, Maggie Garb and Susanna Long, and David Doyle, respectively. Professor Anderson would like to thank Jean Keene of Washington College in Chestertown, Maryland for her skillful preparation of the typescript of the chapter on Aristotle.

We would also like to thank the Instructional Development Center of the University of Vermont for a grant that helped provide time for the beginnings of this work. John Clarke deserves special mention for the encouragement which he has given us during the past several years.

R. Thomas Simone would like to express his gratitude to his parents, Reno and Norma Simone, for their unfailing concern and guidance. He dedicates his work on this book to them.

Richard Sugarman would like to express his appreciation to Leah, whose encouragement and assistance have enabled him to go forward with his work. In esteem and gratitude his portion in this book is dedicated to her.

# Contents

# *Preface*

In *Reclaiming the Humanities* we present a considered reading of what we believe to be at the core of the Western tradition of thought: Homer, the tragedians, Plato, Aristotle, and the Bible. Necessarily, we have had to exercise a great deal of selectivity even within our individual chapters, but each section of this work offers an interpretation of a major figure through discussion of seminal texts. The overarching theme of our approach is that an engagement with both the Greek and Biblical traditions is essential both to the modern quest for self-knowledge and to a responsible concept of education in the contemporary world.

The chapters which follow were conceived as parts of a mosaic of the origins of our cultural tradition rather than as a seamless traversal of all Greek and Biblical thought. While this book is most profitably read as a whole, it has been authored in such away that each chapter has its own integrity and may be read witout presupposing the rest. To help in such reading we have suggested various works in the critical literature that have proved to be influential and original in grappling with the most important early texts in the West.

This work is itself the product of an ongoing dialogue between the authors carried out in the presence of their students, mentors, colleagues, and friends, but in the end primarily with themselves. It represents an attempt to reclaim the legacy of the Humanities, whose future we believe is prefigured in its beginnings. It is but one of many approaches to the human subject, whose study, in a broad sense, is called the Humanities. The focus of our inquiry begins with an awareness of the unintended consequences that follow from the division of knowledge into discrete disciplines. This division dramatically increases the clarity and power of analysis but culminates in the fragmenting of the study of the human subject in our own times.

If we have tarried overlong on Homer, it is because we believe that his place within the Humanities has been understated and become, as have literature, philosophy, and religion in general, the province of specialists. Further, if we have not traced out the historical development of the Biblical world into the normative religions of the West, it is because we believe that this prior encounter between the root traditions of the West must first be reanimated. Our reflections are thematic rather than historical in character. The questions which we would bring to the texts are timely, and in certain cases exigent. To preserve textual fidelity within an existential appoach risks anachronism. Still, while the texts are situated in contexts of their own, their enduring power and meaning necessitate an encounter which is weighted by the concerns of this historical hour.

'Reclaiming the humanities' is a task with infinite horizons, a reflection that takes on content in the realm of idea and speech, but which in the last analysis is confirmed by the action of dialogue as well as the contemplation of mind. Such work aims neither at being encyclopedic nor exclusive. The study of the Greek and Biblical worlds needs to be deepened before it is expanded, appreciated before it is thematized, and studied together with others where all are in the position of learners and the texts themselves become our teachers.

*Burlington, Vermont*
*August 28, 1985*

RECLAIMING THE HUMANITIES

Chapter One

# THE HUMANITIES, ANCIENT AND MODERN

## I. The Humanities and Nietzsche's Syllabus

Our approach in this book is to present a contemporary and radically grounded introduction to the humanities. Within the context of the modern university the various areas of academic disciplines have been divided into three broad areas: the sciences, the social sciences, and the humanities. The sciences treat the understanding of the physical world around us; the social sciences treat social organization through objective methodology; and the humanities treat those areas of study that include languages, literature, arts, and the qualitative study of human existence in fields such as philosophy and religion. The nature of the humanities has been much debated in recent years, and under the pressure of the advance of the technological world within and surrounding the university, the humanities have been subject to significant criticism. This is particularly the case as the university has become more and more vocational. Even the unity of the humanities has become an issue for debate. However, the area of the humanities represents the origin and major history of education in the West since the age of the ancient Greeks.

The concept and history of the humanities derive from the Latin word *humanitatis*, which means in its broad sense the study of human nature. The term was used by Cicero to indicate the education that was necessary for the preparation of an ideal orator--the ideal orator being a politically and culturally mature individual. Thus, the Latin word *humanitatis* can mean both 'humanity' and a special kind of education.

1

# RECLAIMING THE HUMANITIES

The word *humanitatis*, according to one ancient source, is a Latin translation of the Greek word *paideia*. In ancient Greece *paideia* was the process of the general and liberal education used in preparing a person for adulthood and for civic freedom and responsibility. Thus, the origin of the idea of the humanities is connected with a broad kind of study that both introduces a student to culture in general and to the student's own growing competence as an autonomous individual within that culture.

In the age of Pericles in ancient Athens schools came into being in order to to carry out a program of *paideia* concentrating on a number of areas of study that became the core of higher education for more than 2000 years. The concept of *paideia* in the Periclean age, according to Georges Gusdorf, "denoted a complete education based on grammatical correctness and intellectual accuracy in dialectical thinking, with the molding of the adult's personality as a goal."[1] These early educators taught seven 'arts' that presented a comprehensive view of the world. In medieval times these arts became known as the trivium and the quadrivium, an arrangement of the seven arts of education into groups of three and four areas, respectively. The trivium included the literary subjects: grammar, rhetoric, and dialectics. The quadrivium included the scientific subjects: arithmetic, geometry, harmony, and astronomy. While some of these subjects might seem narrow to a modern eye, they actually included a great deal of broad theoretical and reflective training. The common themes of *paideia* and *humanitatis* were the ideas of a shared cultural human nature and the leading of the student into maturity and civic responsibility. This was true both in the classical world of Greece and Rome and in the Christian middle ages, permitting a transformed under-standing of the essence of human nature modified by an encounter with Biblical sources.

With the Renaissance rediscovery of the classical world, a renewed appreciation both of the ancient world and of the powers of

# The Humanities, Ancient and Modern

humans as opposed to the powers of a religious world view based on Christianity began to emerge. These scholars and teachers called themselves the Humanists. These 'humanists' based their study on the culture and history of ancient Greece and Rome and devoted great effort to the restoration and elucidation of ancient texts. Along with this study of ancient texts came a sense of the renewed intellectual capabilities of human beings. After the provincial segmenting of Europe during the middle ages, the rebirth of humanistic scholarship made available for the educated a rich cultural tradition of literature, mythology, and history. The powerful new imagery of the ancient world became truly relevant and contemporary in the eyes of modern artists such as Shakespeare, Monteverdi, and Goethe. Classical stories and myths became, as in Shakespeare's *Antony and Cleopatra*, vibrant modern creation.

Parallel to the influence and model of the Renaissance humanists and their legacy for the culture of the West was the new rationalistic orientation of science. Beginning with Copernicus' new mathematical reordering of the world picture, the inductive methods of science and the mathematical analysis of the material world came into greater and greater influence. Thus by the time of the 18th century there were two broad areas of academic inquiry standing side by side: the cultural studies of the Humanists, based largely on ancient authors, and the rationalistic studies of science, based on experimental observation and mathematical description of the physical world. These were the new arts and sciences that make up the core of the general education aspect of the modern university.

The development of nineteenth and twentieth century education has been the growth of rational investigation not just of physical nature but also of social activity, which has become the social sciences, and also of language, literature, art, history, and philosophy, which are, in a broad sense, the modern humanities. In addition, the humanities came to concern themselves not just with the ancient world and its authors and history but also with the works and culture of the modern world.

The strength of rational investigation has been an analytic method, which is to say a separation into parts. An unintended consequence of the rationalistic dominance in the modern university has been to foster both a profound division not only between the disciplines, but even more importantly, between knowledge and existence. While the individual disciplines of the humanities have their pre-professional aspects, the strength of the humanities in their broad context is to encourage a concerted reflection on the image and meaning of human nature. Part of the implication of this reflection is the interrelation of various kinds of study and the ideal of the human being within a cultural context and as an intellectually and morally sound individual. This emphasis on the interrelatedness of knowledge and on the development of the individual is central to our perspective in this book.

Toward the middle of the nineteenth century an incipient rebellion against Western rationalism began to call into question the separation between knowledge and existence. Nietzsche and Kierkegaard, two of the greatest modern students of the Greek and Biblical worlds respectively, began to challenge rationalistic abstraction against the claims and needs of lived existence. Man was becoming problematic to himself. The crisis of contemporary education is precisely the division between abstract learning and the knowledge that a learner has of his own existence.

Our stance in this book, drawn from Nietzsche and Kierkegaard and from our own teaching and thinking, calls for a new and authentic encounter with the seminal texts of the Western world. Nietzsche and Kierkegaard were two of the most astute critics of the contradictions that face modern man. It was not by accident that Kierkegaard focussed on Socrates in the Greek tradition and on the figure of the Biblical Abraham in order to address the roots of his own existential crisis. Our approach to the origins of the West is an existential one based on the insights into contemporary life of some of the most original of modern thinkers.

Nietzsche's own syllabus, offered when he was the youngest full professor ever appointed to a European university, extended from Homer to Aristotle. As Heidegger, Nietzsche's most formidable expositor, observes, before one tackles Nietzsche in earnest, one must undertake to study what Nietzsche studied and adds for emphasis that it is best to spend fifteen years working through Aristotle before opening a text of Nietzsche's. What Heidegger knew and what Nietzsche knew even better, was that the crises and catastrophes of the twentieth century were encoded in the dynamic possibilities of the ruling beginnings of the West. It is here in Nietzsche's view, in the dawn of human understanding that the existential agenda of the West is set in motion.

## *The Odyssey* and Education

The process of education is from its root an odyssey of discovery, a journey to find ourselves through the paths that have been united in us and in our world. The word 'odyssey' is deliberately chosen for its specific and general origin. For the word-concept 'odyssey' derives its dynamism from the emblematic man in search of the meaning of existence first described by Homer. Our own search for self-understanding is a collective as well as a personal pursuit. Necessarily, then, such an odyssey must retrace the turns by which we, as the subjects of our own enquiry, have been thrust into the con-temporary world through ancient adventures. Our goal is not to engage in antiquarian history, for to do so, we should remain one with the artifacts unearthed. Rather, our true task is to make those ancient odysseys live again, and thereby to install the past in the present. To do so will make us contemporary with our own collective beginnings, and consequently throw a light ahead of ourselves where future, past, and present are stilled long enough to let us think along with our teachers, the texts themselves.

To think in a vacuous space is permitted only to mystics who have neither origins nor ends. Timely thinking moves through a space inhabited by texts. Homer's *Odyssey* is a signal text of the ancient Greek world that bears the signature of its central figure. Through measured reading we learn to encounter with Odysseus the world as it looked to him.

In Book Nine of Homer's *Odyssey* the wandering hero is honored at a banquet by the Phaiakians in his last stop before his long delayed return to his home and family in Ithaka. As entertainment at the banquet the bard Phemios sings stories about the gods and the heroes at Troy. Odysseus, after a heartfelt response to the story of the Trojan horse, turns to thank his host and to begin his own marvelous narrative of adventure and testing. He sums up the summer evening, the food, and especially the art of the poet in these words, as interpreted by Robert Fitzgerald:

> There is no boon in life more sweet, I say,
> than when a summer joy holds all the realm,
> and banqueters sit listening to a harper
> with bread and roast meat, while a steward goes
> to dip up wine and brim your cups again.
> Here is the flower of life, it seems to me![2]

Odysseus, as the first cultured man--Joyce called him the first gentleman in Europe--directs our attention to the fruits of life and complements his experience of the struggle to return to home and self identity with an awareness of both beauty and delight. In this as in so many other ways Odysseus is the paradigm, the model of the ways that people in the Western tradition have seen themselves and their world.

The struggle to survive and find an identity, the desire for further experience of the world, a recognition of the physical limits and imaginative expansiveness of man, a capacity for reflection on the world and on human nature along with an appreciation of beauty that human beings can make--these are the most salient of the lessons of Odysseus. And as we are all in many ways members of the family of Odysseus, we too must learn those lessons.

Odysseus was faced with a practical task--the need to return to his home after the rigors of the Trojan war and the ten year long wanderings after the war. His task was one of action. But as Homer reveals to us, the origins of action are not clearly physical and are indeed obscurely hidden in the *ethos* of a character. As we argue in our chapter on Homer, the root of Odysseus' task was the question of his own nature and identity, that is, what is it to be Odysseus or, for that matter, to be a human being? What is the enigma of existence that is to be solved in order for action to take place or have meaning? Where does meaning reside--in action or in character or in neither? Odysseus' task and character are the material of heroic legend, but Homer with unique immediacy captures the way that Odysseus' story is a root story of the problems of human nature. For Homer the story is of the greatest importance, but he exposes for the first time in the secular tradition of the West those themes about meaning and identity that persist to this very day.

Homer's cultural primacy is partly an historical one; his epics are the earliest preserved long stories in our cultural tradition. But the explanation for his primacy goes much deeper. As the creator and preserver of the forms of human life writ large on an epic canvas and with a power of penetration given only to the most radical of figures, Homer both feeds the life that comes after him and draws the curiosity and passion of the most inquisitive thinkers. The development of the West in its secular expression could quite properly be understood as a commentary on Homer. Aeschylus, Plato, Vergil, Dante, Shakespeare, Monteverdi, Vico, Nietzsche, James Joyce--all of these masters have participated in a commentary on Homer. Only by returning to the roots of our world and by participating in a commentary on them can we come to a more educated relationship to our own nature.

## Texts: Reading and Interpreting

The example of Homer is a most rigorous one, and only the most original and perceptive of cultural figures are equal to such a standard. But, in fact, we have a broad consensus within the history of the humanities about the most influential intellectual and cultural origins of our tradition. Homer, the Greek tragedians, the Greek philosophers, the Bible--these are the roots that we concentrate on as the most important. Of course, as our study continues out of the ancient world and closer to the modern world in chronology our selection of texts becomes more diverse. In our approach to our own beginnings and toward our own self understanding, we have adapted the tradition of centering our study on primary early texts and striving to enter into the commentary on these formative figures of our world. Our study is largely based on the idea of the humanities that reaches back to the Periclean Age of ancient Athens. But our approach to the texts begins from a contemporary curiosity and desire to meet ourselves in our own past.

As we approach the important texts that help to form the core of the culture and thought of the West, we become aware of the the difficulties of reading and of interpreting. The texts themselves seem, at first, closed and cryptic, needing the help of contemporary interpretive approaches to liberate their meanings. Just as the script for a drama is but the surface of its life, containing both the multiple intentions from the author and offering limitless recreative possibilities to its director and actors, so the text of a work like *The Odyssey* is a calm surface to be awakened by inquiry, challenge, and interpretation--both to recover the multiplicity of the beginnings and to liberate our own understanding.

8

# The Humanities, Ancient and Modern

The great story of Odysseus' challenge to the Cyclops is an engaging adventure tale. But when we begin to ask about the sources of Odysseus' curiosity and of his belief in his superiority, his disdain for the primitive conditions of the giant, and his haughty retort to the blinded creature, we are impelled to ask how the story contains the hero's cultural and psychological attitudes and whether the author agrees or disagrees with the perspective of his character. In such interpretive inquiry we begin to open up the avenues between ourselves and the text.

Or again, when Odysseus nears the seductive Sirens, women with irresistible voices, who lure sailors onto rocks of destruction, he plugs his men's ears with wax but has his men tie him to the mast as they pass. Under the yearning, engulfing effect of the Sirens' songs, Odysseus begs his men to let him free, but they only bind him tighter and sail deafly on. Surely, this adventure is more than a momentary event of testing, for it calls to us as the deadly maidens called to Odysseus, and we must awake our minds and feelings to the power and possibilities of the events.

## II.  Knowledge and  Self-Knowledge

## 1.  The Riddle of the Sphinx:  The Greek Concept of Knowledge

On his way to Thebes, Oedipus is posed a riddle by the murderous Sphinx, that for us, no less than for him, is to have life and death implications: What walks on four legs in the morning, two legs in the afternoon, and three legs in the evening? Oedipus responds that it is man himself. In the morning of his life, as an infant he crawls upon all fours, in the afternoon at full strength he stands upright on two legs, and in the evening of his life, in his declining years, he walks tentatively with the assistance of a cane.

What does it mean to be human? In image, as well as idea, this remains the central question haunting the literary imagination, firing the philosophic quest, and shaping the religious vision of man in the West from the first stirrings of existential restlessness to the hour in which we live. How much more so is this the case in our own time, when in the words of Nietzsche, the greatest modern student of the ancient Greeks, "we knowers have become most unknown to ourselves." To Nietzsche, the author who penned the phrase "God is dead," the words of Sophocles in the famous chorus from *The Antigone* have an urgent and current echo: "There is nothing that surpasses man in strangeness." How, then, do we knowers become once again known to our own selves? King Oedipus regarded this question as one that dawns upon every man, some later, some earlier, but a question that is nonetheless inescapable:

> Such being my nature, I cannot become something
> else, I cannot give up the search into my origin, I will
> know who I am (1084-85).[3]

The tragic vision of the Greeks as consummated in the desire and fate of Oedipus poses the riddle of our own self-understanding.

Aristotle, in the first words of his central treatise on reality, affirms that this question of self-knowledge is a natural and universal one, "For all men by nature desire to know." In the *Physics* Aristotle designs a lucid and enduring model to provide knowledge of any subject, including man himself. The categories for addressing the multiplicity of knowledge are enunciated in Aristotle's concept of causality. Four causes in all are distinguished. The material cause is that out of which a thing is made. The shaping of an entity is the formal cause. The primary source of change is called the efficient cause. The final cause is the end, that for which a thing exists.

What for Aristotle, then, is man? From the view of material causality, man is is a biological being, organically constituted, with a certain kinship to other animals. All scientific approaches to the question begin here. Oedipus, of course understood this, just as he did the suffering from his swollen foot. Surely, it is not this kind of knowledge of origins which Oedipus seeks out. Rather, he appears to be asking the question where do I come from? As is true of all other human beings, his biological origin comes from his father and mother. What at the first remains mysterious to Oedipus is that he does not know who his parents are. The very mystery of the drama of *Oedipus the King* only begins to be resolved when Oedipus learns, to his horror, that in his not-knowing, he has murdered his father and married his mother. The tragedy of Oedipus is set in motion by the fact that he learns belatedly the painful but essential distinction between character and nature.

The Greek word for character is *ethos,* which stands at the very center of an ethical definition of being human. It is his *ethos* which separates man from all other beings, and therefore, in a formal sense defines him for Sophocles. But for Oedipus, who lives before the advent of Aristotlian categories, such knowledge is gained through tragic testing of his kingly power in relation to that of the gods who rule over him. But the "gods who have no cares themselves," in the words of Homer, are in turn ruled by nature (the Greek word is *physis*), just as it is 'natural' for them to rule mortals.

What is man? The riddle of the sphinx is answered by Oedipus before its implications can be understood. The travail of King Oedipus is to secure a refuge in a world where man can never be completely at home. This is so just because he demands justice and asks for reasons for his existence out of bottomless solitude. He must in the last analysis provide the reasons for the justice he seeks. In the world of the Tragic Greeks, the gods will not help, because they cannot themselves know anything other than the limits which *physis* mandates for the immortal ones. Offending the *ethos* of the moral order is comprehensible by the gods, and they punish accordingly. However, in a world which they do not create, the gods cannot accommodate the infinite demands of finite beings. To what end then does man aim? This, for Aristotle, is *eudaimonia*, happiness. Unlike Aristotle, Sophocles withholds happiness as an answer for Oedipus. This mortal king must live with the knowledge that he is destined to walk on three legs in the evening, and grope his way to truth.

## 2. The Tree of Life and the Tree of the Knowledge of Good and Evil: The Biblical Concept of Knowledge

"What is man that thou takest cognizance of him?" This is the question the psalmist asks. In the very first psalm of King David, we find the words "Happy is the man who meditates on your law day and night." With these words another vision of the human condition opens up before us. It is the non-tragic world of the Bible. From its root branches the religious life of the West. The contrast with the tragic world of the ancient Greeks is evident in the opening words of King David, sweet singer of Israel. Before the riddle of human existence can be posed, the answer is already advanced: "Before you ask, I shall answer" (Isaiah). The silhouette of man sketched out by the psalmist uses imagery that recalls the riddle of the sphinx. The psalm speaks of sitting, standing, walking. Who is the happy man? He is the one who is upright before God.

> Happy is the man that hath not walked in the counsel of
>     the wicked,
> Nor stood in the way of sinners,
> Nor sat in the seat of the scornful.[4]

From what does his happiness come? "But his delight is in the law of the Lord; and in his law doth he meditate day and night." The word for walk in Hebrew is *Halak* from which the word for Law (*Halakah*) derives. The way to walk becomes known to man through meditation and study of the law of the Torah. In advance of experience knowledge is given. What the tragic Oedipus learns belatedly, his place in the cosmos, is for Hebraic man made known to him from the beginning. For Hebraic man the work of becoming human involves more than finding one's place in the cosmos. It is not an odyssey which

12

involves the search for home and self-restoration. Rather, it is the journey out of the self toward a "land that I will show thee" (Genesis 12).

The non-tragic world of the Hebraic Bible springs from a concept of knowledge, man, world, and God, radically different than that of the Greeks. The confident pronouncement of David is more than a merely different rhetorical model containing the same essential content:

> And he shall be like a tree planted by streams of water,
> that bringeth forth its fruit in its season,
> And whose leaf doth not wither;
> And in whatsoever he doeth
> he shall prosper.          (Psalm 1)

Man is likened to a tree of the field. He is, however, a created being. In his origins are preserved the promise of existence. The concepts of *physis* and nature are not ultimate in the Biblical schemata. Rather, the world itself is created for the sake of of being known. It is the tree of knowledge from which original knowledge is acquired. Unless, the latency of such knowledge were given, it could not become manifest and known. The logic of the created world is accessible to man. It is made known through the medium of a text, the Torah or the Bible. This is why David says he shall meditate on the words of the Torah day and night. Moreover, the Torah is itself referred to as an *etz chaim*, a tree of life.

There is an intimate connection between knowledge and mortality drawn from the opening of Genesis. There are two trees planted in the primal paradise: the tree of the knowledge of good and evil and the tree of immortality. The Biblical narrative focuses on the Tree of Knowledge. From the outset knowledge concerns the most essential kind of value or morality, that of good and evil. Here, in the dawn of human understanding, we are far removed from contemporary oppositions between fact and value, psychology and morality, the physical and the humane sciences. The Biblical concept of knowledge embraces derivative and emerging division. Eating from the tree of the knowledge of good and evil opens human eyes to the divine-human encounter. Thus commences the education of man by God. The Latin word *educere* means to lead out of, and it is in a two-fold sense that God leads man out of innocence into experience and out of immediacy into history.

It is of the greatest significance that in the Biblical presentation of creation the tree of knowledge is encountered before the tree of immortality. Why does the concept of knowledge precede that of immortality? The question is all the more troubling when we reflect upon the fact that the tree of immortality is not forbidden. The knowledge of death enters the world only with the gaining of self-consciousness and the end of innocence. Such knowledge of good and evil signifies a cognizance of the latent opposition within all things, order and disorder. According to Martin Buber,

> The knowledge acquired by man through eating the miraculous fruit is of an entirely different kind. A superior-familiar encompassing of opposites is denied to him who, despite his 'likeness' to God, has a part only in that which is created and not in creation, is capable only of begetting and giving birth, not of creating. Good and evil, the yes-position and the no-position of existence, enter into his living cognizance; but in him they can never be temporally co-existent. Such temporal co-existence, when past, present, and future are indivisible belongs only to the Creator. The created being is bounded by the time in which he finds himself and by the space which he inhabits, which, thereby, become his perspective on the world.[5]

This is why the psalmist says "in his Torah he meditates day and night." The Torah given at Sinai is the instruction that prepares knowledge in advance of experience. Everything that a person needs to know in order to live well is made known to him. His task consists simply in this: to learn from the Teacher and to act in accordance with the

14

instruction. Against the Greek concept of knowledge is counterposed the affirmation that there is a Teacher of all teachers and a text of all texts.

There are several specific ways in which the Biblical concept of knowledge differs dramatically from that of tragic-philosophic tradition of the Greeks. First, in the Biblical world knowledge is exoteric rather esoteric. That is to say, it is public, rather than private. For example, the instruction not to murder would be absurd if it were accompanied by the admonition to keep such knowledge hidden or secret. Consider: "Thou shall not murder (but keep it a secret)." Secondly, the concept of knowing for Biblical man is, for the most part, democratic rather than elitist. While even the Platonic Socrates spends his time primarily in the company of the well-born, well-bred young men of ancient Athens, the Torah of Moses is addressed to every one, even to the hewers of wood and the drawers of water. The text states specifically, this Torah is not in the heavens above nor across the seas, but very close to you, as close as you are to your selves. In the third place, the primary interrogative of the Bible is 'who' rather than 'what.' Human beings are irrevocably personal. Hence, even the transmission of generations is documented with the names of individuals and their offspring. The text is not a book of ideas where personal life is subordinated to conceptual schemes. Biography is the production of existence, ideas the reflective imitations of actions.

There is a fourth discernible difference between the Biblical concept of knowledge and the Greek-philosophic stance. The psalmist, Moses, makes this clear when he asks: "Teach us to number our days that we may get us a heart of wisdom." The affirmation is that there is a mathematics of existence as well as a calculus of things. Generalities must be brought down into the realm of everydayness where walking, sitting, sleeping and standing embody the kind of knowledge that is both open and timely to a creature of flesh and blood.

# RECLAIMING THE HUMANITIES

The kind of knowledge possessed by King Oedipus and Socrates on the one hand, and King David and Moses on the other is not merely additive or quantitative. King David has no advantage over Oedipus when it comes to ruling a people, save one. He suffers the kind of loneliness and torment that comes from being king. Every psalm of the sweet-singer of Israel testifies to this fact. Rather, unlike Oedipus whom the gods tell what they will when they will, if they know, King David recognizes that he is, in the end, not utterly alone. This is a crucial distinction. To be alone means that every great-souled Greek must claim the mantle of divinity, not merely to appear god-like, but to act after the fashion of god himself. The hero fashions self-understanding out of the materials of his own experience. King David, on the other hand is answerable to a law not of his own making. It is, in fact, a Biblical law that the king keep within his possession at all times a scroll of the Divine instruction given at Sinai. He is, like every one of his subjects, answerable before a law that he cannot himself change. Hence, it is not surprising that David responds to the admonition of the prophet, Nathan, when David is chastised in the rare moment in which he errs. How different is David's response before Nathan from that of Oedipus before Teiresias.

The knowledge given to Biblical man does not require that he engage in the super-human task of fashioning himself into a divinity. Rabbi Tarfon used to say: "The day is short; the task is great; the workmen are lazy; the reward is great; and the Master is insistent." Insistent, but not asking of human beings more than he created them capable of attaining: "He used to say: 'You are not called upon to complete the work (of Torah study), yet you are not free to refrain from it.'" This is why King David, who according to Rabbinic legend kept a lyre suspended above his bed, would "wake the dawn" to meditate on the Torah  day and night.

While *The Iliad* is rightly called the Bible of the Greeks, what a different kind of text we find in the Hebraic Bible. Here, God is said to reveal himself in the words of the text. Where is God? God is in the Torah. In this most sublime of all texts, the work of man is joined with that of divinity. Just as the Homeric texts have an oral tradition, the Hebraic Bible has an oral tradition. The difference consists in the fact that the oral tradition of the Bible is an instructional manual for the reading and interpreting of the text.

## III. A Study of the Greek and Biblical Worlds

We have made a necessary selection in our reflections on texts and thinkers from the possibilities of the Greek and Biblical traditions in our discussions in this volume. We place a strong emphasis on the interrelatedness of disciplines, especially of literature, philosophy, and religion. It would be foolhardy to think that we were able to encompass the full complexity of any of our chosen authors or works, but we have proceeded on the assumption that a purposefully chosen path through the origins of the Western tradition would allow the reader to branch out onto other self-selected paths.

In the Greek tradition we give pride of place to Homer. The bold images of the Homeric world and the fullness of feeling and experiential immediacy in the epics seem to us virtually unparalleled in the Western cultural tradition. Further, the dual significance of the stories of Achilles and Odyssey prepares us for the implications of Greek tragedy and philosophy. Like the rosy-fingered dawn of each Homeric day, *The Iliad* and *The Odyssey* have a capacity for renewal that demands that they be encountered in one's life as early and as often as possible.

The tragedians, especially Aeschylus and Sophocles, develop out a Homeric context. The *Oresteia* makes significantly more sense if a reading of it begins against the backdrop of *The Iliad*. Likewise, Sophocles' honed tragedy of character takes on greater meaning against the tragic possibilities of Homer's portrayal of Achilles. The method of tragic dialogue also brings us close to the dialectical oppositions of Plato's Socrates.

In selecting from the work of the great philosophers we have had to attempt to explain through example rather than through the complete analysis of argument and implication. For Plato, a discussion of the *Euthyphro* serves to demonstrate the operation of dialectical method. The presentation of a reading of the *Symposium* reflects the scope and breadth of Platonic thought by showing the dramatic and conceptual unity of a Platonic dialogue. For Aristotle, the themes of purpose and happiness are presented as a distilled core of the whole Aristotelian enterprise. Robert J. Anderson's lucid interpretation of the *Physics* and *Ethics* demonstrates Aristotle's vision of rational understanding that prevails as a model of the relation of nature, reason, and right conduct up to the time of the Enlightenment.

Undoubtedly, the treatment of Biblical material has proved to be the most challenging aspect of our work. The Bible is usually only a passing glance in works dealing with the beginnings of the Western tradition, partly because of doctrinal overlays surrounding the material, partly because of the unparalleled richness and variety of the text. We argue in this volume that the Biblical world is equal in importance and influence to the Greek world. We offer an unusual but, we hope, fertile introduction to the power and contemporary significance of the Biblical vision of human existence. The interpretation of the themes of time and freedom in the Bible presents, we believe, a glimpse of the still unfolding meaning of that central root of the Western intellectual and spiritual tradition.

Alison Mahoney

# The Humanities, Ancient and Modern

## NOTES

[1]Gusdorf, "Humanistic Scholarship," *Encyclopedia Britannica* (Chicago, 1978), Macropedia, v. 8, p. 1171. This Britannica article is the most convenient version in English of Gusdorf's landmark studies in the history and theory of education.

[2]*The Odyssey* (New York: Doubleday, 1961), p. 160.

[3]*Oedipus Tyrannus,* (New York: Norton, 1970).

[4]Quotations from the Bible are taken from *The Hebrew Scriptures* (Philadelphia: Jewish Publication Society, 1948).

[5]Martin Buber, *Good and Evil* (New York: Schocken, 1954), p.75.

Chapter Two

# THE NATURAL ETHIC OF THE HOMERIC WORLD

At the very beginning of the Western tradition stand two texts of incomparable power and depth, the Hebraic Bible and the Homeric epics. While other texts like the *Gilgamesh* may come earlier, they have not attained either the defining authority or the continuous currency of the Bible and Homer. While the theologies of these two bodies of work differ essentially, both share in a passionate vision that places man at the center of a world that can yield, however painfully, a full sense of human meaning and purpose. Readers for tens of centuries have found that these texts in their different ways have captured the fullness of human nature with unparalleled directness and suggestiveness.

The Homeric epics as we have them today seem to be much as they were for the Greeks of 5th century Athens. The poems look back to the Mycenaean Greek world of 1500 to 1000 B.C.E. and the warrior kings of the small city-states of that era, but the process of story telling and language are the products of the somber time that followed the Dorian invasions and the destruction of Golden Mycenae, that period from 1000 to 650 B.C.E. called the Dark Age of Greece. During the Dark Age not only were economic wealth and political coherence lost but the ability to write was lost as well. According to recent theories, an oral-formulaic story telling emerged during this time and developed great richness of language and subject matter from the myths of the war at Troy and the consequently troubled return home of the Greek heroes. Our *Iliad* and *Odyssey* are the distillations and perfections of that kind of poetry and that era.

## RECLAIMING THE HUMANITIES

A debate has raged since the late eighteenth century over the question: who was Homer? The many repetitions of language and certain inconsistencies in the poems led many to postulate a patch work quilt model of composition, but for many, if not most scholars, the oral-formulaic theories, first advanced by Milman Parry in the 1930s, have shown the rational probability of single authorship for each poem. And it would not be wrong to allow tradition and sentiment to convince us that the composer of *The Iliad* was also the composer of *The Odyssey*.

With the opening of *The Iliad* , the first enduring literary moment of our tradition, Homer plunges us into a world of dramatic power and a certain simplicity of character but also into a world tormented by issues and passions that plague us to this day. *The Iliad* is avowedly about rage: "Sing, Muse, the wrath of Achilles, son of Peleus." The setting is the siege of Troy, where the assembled Greek heroes have come to exact vengeance for the abduction of Menelaos' beautiful wife, Helen, by Paris, son of King Priam of Troy. The central figure of the poem is angry Achilles, greatest of the Greeks in warlike power, yet thwarted in his desire for glory, as we see almost immediately, by the political power of Agamemnon, leader of the Greek host. As we learn only a little while later, the frustration of personal honor reveals Achilles' tragic dilemma: he can choose a long life at peace without honor or a short life with great honor. Either way, even Achilles, greatest in prowess among men, must die.

Thus, at the very dawn of Western consciousness are the inescapable questions of the life and death of civilized existence as imaged in the destruction of a city and all personal worth in the face of mortality. What is so remarkable about Homer is his ability to summon the most complete associations through telling the most direct possible stories. The range and immediateness of events in the opening book of *The Iliad* present us with a completeness and memorableness seldom, if ever, equalled in later literature. In the story stand strange figures, an Achilles, an Agamemnon, a Helen, who are mysteriously close to us and our psyches.

## I.  Heroism and the Destruction of the City:  Homer's *Iliad*

The confrontation between Achilles and Agamemnon in Book One of *The Iliad* is posed for us by Homer as a quarrel of truly Olympian proportions. The greatest of warriors has been insulted by a man who is his admitted inferior in battle and yet who not only rules over him, but is by definition accorded the stature of being the greatest of men. After King Agamemnon is revealed as having brought a plague upon the Greeks, he is confronted with the necessity of returning a prize possession acquired in battle waged for, but apparently not by, him. Calchas, the fortune-teller who has foreseen the sequence of events, asks the brave Achilles for protection if he is to bring this matter before the council of Greek warriors.  Achilles reassures him, challenges Agamemnon to return his prize, the daughter of a priest of Apollo, and thus end the plague.  This insults the king's authority with the result that Agamemnon threatens to take Achilles' own prize, Briseis of the lovely cheeks, or perhaps the prize of Ajax, strongest of the Greeks, or the prize of the ever-ready Odysseus. Achilles alone responds to the provocation of Agamemnon.  Odysseus is a man who knows when to remain silent.  Ajax, whose strength may not be matched by his wit, appears not to know that he has been insulted.

For Achilles the situation is intolerable.  If he, the greatest of warriors, can be injured by such a mean-spirited gesture, then pride is subject to the demands of reflection.  The scheme of glory that rises as magnificently and as naturally as the rosy-fingered dawn can be covered by gray clouds of self doubt, which is, after all, the beginning of consciousness.  Achilles has become problematic to himself, an opening onto reflection, in a world where the heroic resolve to carry through what one has promised alone measures man. As Achilles withdraws from the battle and the public code of honor, he sets himself apart in action and in mind. Homer probes his indomibitable solitude, until the hero can rejoin and in a way of tragic irony confirm the heroic world.

The oath that Achilles makes in Book One not to return to battle until the Greeks eat their hearts out with remorse and fall in their hundreds to Hektor, killer of men, sets in motion a course of action that leads to his absence from the battlefield and the suspension of time in which the decision to reconstitute the meaning of his world from a reflective stance is made:

> "But I will tell you this and swear a great oath upon it:
> in the name of this sceptre, which never again will bear leaf
> nor branch, now that it has left behind the cut stump in the mountains,
> nor shall it ever blossom again, since the bronze blade stripped
> bark and leafage, and now at last the sons of the Achaians
> carry it in their hands in state when they administer
> the justice of Zeus. And this shall be a great oath before you:
> some day longing for Achilleus will come the sons of the Achaians,
> all of them. Then stricken at heart though you be, you will be able
> to do nothing, when in their numbers before man-slaughtering Hector
> they drop and die. And then you will eat out the heart within you
> in sorrow, that you did no honor to the best of the Achaians."
>
> (BOOK I, ll. 233-244)[1]

Book One of *The Iliad* presents in microcosm the world of Homeric man and the conflict within Achilles that makes it possible for the hearer of the poem to assume a critical distance from it.

24

# Homer

The wrath of Achilles is, in the first instance, directed against Agamemnon. The collision of the two heroes is an occassion for reflecting upon the relation of power to justice. Achilles, who has been treated unjustly now cloaks himself in the mantle of justice. He will be as upright and unbending as the sceptre which he holds and by which he makes his vow not to return to battle. Nowhere in *The Iliad* is there a single view on the justice of the war between the Greeks and the Trojans provided by Homer, or on the nature of peace as over against war. The tasks of war and destruction, in the service of force are given treatment, as Simone Weil notes, in the description of the terror which confronts every man who perishes on the plains of Ilium.[2] Unhesitatingly Achilles, by his oath, dooms his comrades and foes alike. For a short time, however, he spares himself. We should remember that the entire drama is but a depiction of the twilight of the war, taking only forty-nine days. Achilles retires to his ships to be with his beloved companion Patroklus, to play upon his lyre, to watch the battle from afar, to brood, and as we learn, to think critically about a world in which he, its fiercest emblem, cannot be accepted without sorrow, rage, and resentment. The playful world where gods and mortals interact with grace, gaiety, festive celebration, and deeds of nobility is finally death-dealing, filled with illusion that is bound up with impenetrable appearances and the anarchic.

The figure of the solitary Achilles is set in more acute relief by Hektor whose father, King Priam, knows the comfort of his presence, and by Andromache, his wife, to whom Hektor serves as husband, father, and brother, and most poignantly by Astyanax, his small son, frightened for a moment by his father's forbidding bronze armor but succoured by his fatherly embrace that greets him in respite from battle. In contrast to Hektor, Achilles is solitary, alone, and abandoned. In Book Nine of *The Iliad* the surrogates of Agamemnon entreat, encourage, and scold Achilles for not returning to war. The ambassadors are warmly greeted, yet in the end powerfully and

disturbingly rejected.  Odysseus and Ajax are accompanied by the aged
Phoenix, tutor of the young Achilles, whom Peleus, the absent father
of Achilles, has sent before him to be a guide and companion.  Achilles
questions the sincerity of Agamemnon, the depth to which his oath has
been fulfilled; and in a moment far removed from the immediate
concerns of the emissaries, he challenges the worth of war, honor, and
bravery, the very stuff from which Homeric man is fashioned.

Now we learn that the choice of destinies set for him by nature and
not Agamemnon alone has occasioned the wrath of Achilles:

> "For not
> worth the value of my life are all the possessions they fable
> were won for Ilion, that strong-founded citadel, in the old
>     days
> when there was peace, before the coming of the sons of the
>     Achaians...
> ...a man's life cannot come back again, it cannot be lifted
> nor captured again by force, once it has crossed the teeth's
>     barrier.
> For my mother Thetis the goddess of the silver feet tells me
> I carry two sorts of destiny toward the day of my death.
> Either,
> if I stay here and fight beside the city of the Trojans,
> my return home is gone, but my glory shall be everlasting;
> but if I return home to the beloved land of my fathers,
> the excellence of my glory is gone, but there will be a long
>     life
> left for me, and my end in death will not come to me quickly.
> And this would be my counsel to others also, to sail back
> home again, since no longer shall you find any term set
> on the sheer city of Ilion, since Zeus of the wide brows has
> held his own hand over it, and its people are made bold."
>                                   (BOOK IX, ll. 400-420)

Achilles' anger is directed against a dual destiny, which poses
unacceptable alternatives.  To meet death in the morning of his life is
the prohibitive cost of the legendary heroism associated with his name.

# Homer

To leave the battle for tranquility is to devalue the indisputable excellence of glory. The decision to embrace his destiny is made with the full weight of death's finality held in view.

In the first response to the overture of Odysseus to return, Achilles accuses Agamemnon of being a double-dealer and an ingrate:

> "For as I detest the doorways of Death, I detest that man, who
> hides one thing in the depths of his heart, and speaks forth another.
> But I will speak to you as seems best to me: neither
> do I think the son of Atreus, Agmemmnon, will persuade me,
> nor the rest of the Danaans, since there was no gratitude given
> for fighting incessantly against your enemies."
>
> (BOOK IX, ll. 312-317)

Yet, these same themes of duplicity, ingratitude, and futility of heroic toil are tacitly ascribed to a more formidable foe than Agamemnon:

> "Fate is the same for the man who holds back, the same if he fights hard.
> A man dies still if he has done nothing, as one who has done much."
>
> (BOOK IX, ll 318-320)

The devaluation of heroic striving by the force of nature's fated necessity undergirds Achilles' reproach to Agamemnon. Beating within the breast of Achilles is the fear of every man, then and now, that the end of life can signal the end of meaning. Surely, the uncaring immortals are as unwilling as they are unable to alter such a destiny. Who, then, attests to his greatness when the death of the hero makes him deaf to the applause of his admirers?

Withdrawal from the war has given Achilles a breathing-space in which to contemplate a psuedo-decision. The course of his fate has been inscribed in his character. Despite his feint in the direction signalled by the peace of home, this means no exit, but a lengthy pause, which for him, cannot be life's achievement. The action of *The Iliad* envelops him like the whirling eddies of the River Xanthus which he has no real alternative but to fight to the death.

Achilles requires the justification of his mortal and, therefore, human existence in the shape of a necessity that will return him to his natural setting, the battlefield. His return must be accomplished so that his understanding of mortality and honor will be deepened in accordance with his fate, not erradicated. Homer provides him with a strategy to re-enter the theater of self-certainty, which while bearing him away from the reach of the absurd, marks him as the most exemplary of Homeric mortals. Before he can rout the warriors of Troy, his anger must be redirected away from Agamemnon toward Hektor. This is accomplished when Hektor slays Patroklus, beloved friend of Achilles. In the *aristeia* (the showing forth of excellence) of Patroklus, Achilles and Hektor are drawn inexorably toward their climactic encounter, which will mean death for each. Brave each day, Hektor is permitted one last glorious victory when he brings down Patroklus near the gates of Troy. Achilles--having reluctantly consented to Patroklus' donning of his armor to lead his own fresh troops, the Myrmidons, into battle--had cautioned, and perhaps tempted Patroklus towards his death, by forbidding him to go beyond the Scaen gates. For, as he says, the glory of bringing down Hektor and Troy, belong, by destiny, only to Achilles.

Patroklus looks like Achilles to the warriors of Troy, who recoil in horror at his figure. Cutting an unswerving course past the most redoubtable of the warriors of Troy, Patroklus acts like the death-dealing Achilles and to the same destructive effect. Patroklus carries more than the persona of Achilles with him. He bears the possibility of his reflected honor and the certainty of his rendevous with untimely death. The substance of Achilles is greater still than his shadow. The measure of valor and heroic possibility is being counted out. Even with Patroklus, the Myrmidons, and all the Greek men of war on one side, and Achilles alone, on the other, Achilles weighs them down and is greater still. Surely, he could not have risked his lot for Agamemnon, except in an action that would establish his asserted primacy over such a rival. Confirmation of Achilles' victory over Agamemnon must wait until the funeral games for Patroklus when Achilles assumes the mantle of ruler, bestowing recognition, awarding prizes and behaving in the manner one would expect from a king.

It is with fate that Achilles' greatest battle remains to be waged. Human force, however great, cannot overcome what nature has predetermined. In his absence from the battle Achilles has already learned this. To prove worthy of his protectress, Athena, Achilles is forced to adopt her attributes of cunning prudence, the natural companion of military excellence. He knows that the satisfaction of triumph is momentary, that rememberance imitates life in its perishability. He cannot know what the reader does, that the poet will make his achievement immortal. The Greeks, even the greatest among them, proved silent and, therefore, unappreciative when his honor was sullied by Agamemnon. Therefore, he must accomplish in imagination what is withheld from him in the realm of action. He must become the worthy spectator of his own spectacular triumph. This he does by watching a figure who to all appearances is Achilles, and not his alter-ego, Patroklus. Furthermore, Achilles must become the mourner who grieves at his own bier. For, who can understand or value a life lost better than the one who loses it. Achilles fights Hektor twice. Once with mortal armor in the persona of Patroklus and again in the armor divinely crafted by Hephaestus. He dies twice.

Hektor's parting prophesy that Achilles will fall to Paris by the Skaian gates is fulfilled. Homer, however, withholds what should be the thematic finale to the life of Achilles from the reader's sight. For Achilles has let go his dread of death in the instant he hears of the perishing of Patroklus. Resolutely, he fights no longer with his fears, but with his adversaries from Troy: men and demi-gods and, lastly,

Troy's noblest protector. For an instant he blanches after having disgourged the blood of a glut of Trojan warriors in the demi-god River Xanthus. The river, who has called deities to his side, threatens in revenge to engulf Achilles. It is anger, however, that proves more enduring than dread. The death of Hektor cannot placate him.

Day after day he desacrates Hektor's lifeless body, dragging it in the dust about the Achaian camp. His grief for Patroklus is insatiable and suspect in its motive. For Achilles' insane behavior is looked on with dismay by his allies and disapproval by the Olympians. Only when the shade of Patroklus appears to him one black, eerie night and exacts a two-fold promise, does calm begin to prevail in the torn psyche of Achilles. Patroklus asks for his release, that his body be set upon the funeral pyre, and that once consumed, his bones be secured and one day commingled with those of Achilles. Any lingering doubt as to the function of Patroklus in *The Iliad* is put to rest. He and Achilles have been joined by Homer in life, formed into a single destiny with a dual expression.

Vicariously, Achilles has witnessed his triumph, suffered and grieved his death, lamented over his lost possibility, but has not surmounted what fate has decreed as its price. Far from gently does Achilles let the figure of Patroklus go into that dark night. In a last act of horrifying rage he throws twelve living Trojans upon the funeral pyre of Patroklus, and living horses also. In the funeral games for Patroklus we see another side of the life of Achilles, the pacific possibility glimpsed but unrealized. He behaves with kingly equanimity, graciousness, and condescending humor. Homer even permits him to smile.

When Homeric man has no adversaries to wrestle with he makes himself into an adversary and celebrates his victory through contest. His diet does not vary. Meat and wine are his food and drink and contest the wine and meat of his daily regimen. In a fitting note it is through the eyes of Achilles that we behold the excellence of each warrior when the press of war is not upon him. Understandably, Odysseus makes off with most of the prizes. When Helen, together with the leaders of Troy stood in Book Six upon the ramparts and took the measure of each Greek, it was not only in the midst of battle, but also in relation to worth in war. Helen served at the pleasure of Aphrodite, who counts out worth in a different manner than Athena does.

Just because Achilles is the central figure of *The Iliad* we should expect that other mortals would participate in his predicament. *The Odyssey* does not so much parallel *The Iliad* as give evidence of the development of its unrealized possibility. Hektor, not as gifted as Odysseus nor as single-minded as his conqueror, Achilles, nonetheless remains the worthy rival of Achilles in reflection as well as in battle. Achilles has reason to be jealous of Hektor, to wish to possess that lot which has fallen to Hektor. For Hektor, despite his cruel death, has known recognition, honor, heroism, love, affection, and fidelity. Fate, which made him the rival of Achilles, spared him the terrible freedom of an impossible decision in which life would be the slave of honor. Only once does he experience the failure of decision that unmakes a warrior and creates a human being. Encumbered by obligations that are always kept, restrained in his imagination by acute realism, he dwells in the immediacy of action and not in the mode of anticipation. In the climactic turn of *The Iliad*, to which the drama has been building all along, Hektor sees himself in frozen terror in the glittering shield of Achilles. Drawn down to a single, terrible moment are two hands of fate pointing in opposing directions, one toward home and Troy, the embrace of Andromache, his father, Priam, and his little son Astyanax; the other hand pointing away from home toward the inevitable destruction at the pinnacle of heroism in his encounter with Achilles:

> Time after time he has turned the tide of battle, he has
> taken the measure of Ajax and the very gravest of the

RECLAIMING THE HUMANITIES

Achaeans; yet now he, the dawntless, 'leaves and takes to flight.'[3]

He is pictured by Homer as being torn within his shaggy breast. As Rachel Bespaloff says, "Homer wanted him to be a whole man and spared him neither the quaking of terror nor the shame of cowardice." Hektor runs. "And this flight, short as it is, has the eternity of a nightmare." Three times around the world of stone-still Troy Achilles, the swiftfooted, pursues Hektor, who cannot outrun either Achilles or what his fate has decreed. Just as Hektor's fulfilled life has shadowed Achilles as the path he could only glimpse, so too, now the death-dealing doubt which plagued Achilles shadows Hektor's own sense of certainity. For in a moment everything held sacred can be wrested from him.

When in a sudden act of will Hektor regains his composure, he is ready to take his stand against Achilles. The rivals, worthy of one another, favored by the immortals, meet a last time on the plains of perishability. Hektor, who worried that there would be no one to teach his son the spear is, in tragic inversion, to be supplanted by his father, King Priam, reduced to pleading with Achilles for the body of his son. Upon the urging of Hermes, King Priam softens the heart of Achilles by asking him to recall the plight of Peleus, his own father, who will never again have the comfort of seeing his son. In a gesture that links humans together in their bond of mortality, Achilles breaks down, weeping cathartically, now at last, for someone beside himself. Priam, forced to kiss the hands of the man who slaughtered his son, is caught up in the lament expressed by Achilles, who appears to have caught hold of an insight that is the beginning of a full, tragic vision:

> We mortals are wretched beings; the gods who have no cares themselves have woven sorrow into the very fabric of our lives.[4]

The epic then closes the way it opened, with a suppliant asking release of a hostage. This time the booty is not the prize of war, but its victim.

For war creates a world where the survivors also are victims, where suppliants roam the earth, and where fathers live to bury their sons. Homer provides no epilogue to *The Iliad*. The words of another warrior, a poet living in the same epoch but in what one suspects was a different world, are needed: "How are the mighty fallen, and the weapons of war perished!"

## II. The Return to Self and Other: Homer's *Odyssey*

The Homeric world cannot be wholly known from *The Iliad* or *The Odyssey* alone but only from the complement of the two together. Just as the cosmos portrayed by Hephaistos on the Shield of Achilles (*Iliad*, BOOK XVIII) contains two cities of man, one at war and one at peace, so Homer portrays two worlds, one at war in *The Iliad* and one at peace in *The Odyssey*. *The Odyssey* focuses on private, even isolated lives, as humans strive to recreate a viable community after the experience of destruction at Troy and on the ill-fated homecoming of the Achaians. Where *The Iliad* dwells on the moment of death, *The Odyssey* proves the process of survial and the return to life. As with many of the best writers, like Plato or Shakespeare or Tolstoy, so with Homer, comparative reading of his works leads to ever fuller illumination and finer pleasure. *The Odyssey* is usually considered to be the later work, at least it treats a later period of the heroic era than does *The Iliad*, and in the story of Odysseus' wanderings and return there seems to be a subtle but continuous reflection on the war epic.

In *The Poetics* Aristotle distinguishes between the two Homeric poems by calling *The Iliad* an epic of passion (*pathos*) that is simple in form and *The Odyssey* a poem of character (*ethos*) that is complex in form.[5] In essence Aristotle's distinctions are a gloss on the opening lines of each work and on the narrative approaches and thematic concerns of the two poems. The theme of *The Iliad* is the "anger of Achilles," the mode of suffering and tragic passion that derives from Achilles and determines the tone of the entire poem. The subject of

*The Odyssey* is "the man of many turns," the character of Odysseus in all its variety that likewise sets the tone of this poem. As Odysseus is more varied and complex than Achilles, although not so intense, so *The Odyssey* is more varied and complex than *The Iliad* , although not so grand.

Aristotle's distinction between simple and complex points particularly to the recognition scenes so prevalent in *The Odyssey*. Recognition scenes are needed because a conflict has arisen between outer form and inner identity, a conflict symbolized in Odysseus' absence at the beginning of the story. But the arrangement of storytelling in *The Odyssey* is also more artful and complex than in *The Iliad*. Consider that four full books, the famous story of the wanderings, are presented in flashback and through the first person narration of Odysseus himself. Also, note that for four entire books at the opening of *The Odyssey*, the main character is completely absent from the action. These observations only begin to suggest the range of the distinction between simple and complex in the two poems.

*The Odyssey* takes place ten years after the fall of Troy with all of the Greek heroes accounted for either by their return home or by their destruction during the dangerous return voyages. Only Odysseus has neither returned nor been found among the dead. The poem first shows us his absence from the world of family and home and then his return, but Homer also reveals through Odysseus' great narration of his voyages the events of his absence and the reasons for his long delay. The tone of the epic of return is more sensuous and varied than that of the war epic. Fantasy and the fabulous lands of the wanderings color the story as do threatening or cheering natural prospects. Great deeds are done in *The Odyssey* and great dangers passed, but the poem combines adventure story with the achievement and appreciation of the fruits of peace and family. Odysseus' compliment to his Phaiakain hosts typefies this appreciation of daily existence in the poem. While *The Odyssey* embodies the wisdom that life entails pain, a struggle against forces that would drown us in eternal forgetfulness, the poem has the scope and ease to allow for human enjoyment of the fruits of existence.

As we learn from our reading of *The Iliad,* for the Homeric heroes life contains reality and positive being, and death is the negation of all such good. Only a pallid, pathetic shadow of a human being will survive the blow of death. In *The Odyssey* all characters are exposed to a natural ethic in which the embrace of pain yields existence and the ignoring of pain gives oblivion and nothingness. And while this natural ethic applies to the indulgent suitors of Odysseus' wife, Penelope, and to the careless companions of Odysseus, this test of reality applies with even greater force to the hero himself. As George Dimock shows us, the poem is full of choices between pain and numbness, exposing oneself to wounds or cloaking oneself in forgetfullness.[6] The action of the story shows the process of Odysseus' gradual emergence from hiding into a world of danger, where he can ultimately reclaim his identity which had been covered up and almost extinguished.

*The Odyssey* begins enigmatically. Where *The Iliad* plunges into the passion of the quarrel that releases the anger of Achilles, *The Odyssey* starts with the absence of the hero. For the first four books Odysseus is everywhere sought but nowhere found, and his absence from the life-filled narrative implies his absence from existence itself. The characters we first meet are figures who could both derive meaning from Odysseus and grant him meaning if he were present: the son, Telemachos, searching for his maturity; the wife, Penelope, trying to stave off the impertinent suitors and to remember her lost husband; the goddess Athena, wiliest of the immortals, trying to secure her favorite's release; and the safely returned battle companions, old Nestor and Menelaos, nostalgic about the great days of the war.

We finally encounter Odysseus in Book Five crying on the shore of Kalypso's island. As we learn, of his ten years' absence from the world of mortals, three years were spent in fabulous adventures, but fully seven years have been passed on the island of the sea nymph Kalypso. The sojourn with Kalypso is the abyss of non-being into which Odysseus has fallen. While the pleasure of the nymph's paradisal island and her own comely person are powerful allures, Odysseus' detention entails a disturbing withdrawal from dangerous life. Shipwreck on her island is the last event of the wanderings, and leaving the island is the first event of Odysseus' return to life. But unlike the other episodes, which Odysseus narrates with relish, the stay with Kalypso does not have the status of either adventure or event. Rather, it is a kind of limbo, too painless to be real, too impalpable to be confronted. When we hear the hero's narration of his wanderings, we find that some physical and spiritual trauma has engulfed Odysseus, much as the sea has engulfed so many of his companions. The dalliance with Kalypso hides a great fear.

*The Odyssey*, as an epic action, begins with the rejection of Kalypso and the empowerment of Odysseus to leave her island. After the epic proeme, which presents the theme of the poem, the action of *The Odyssey* commences with a council on Olympus where Athena secures Zeus's consent to allow Odysseus's release from Kalypso's island. In one of his many narrative finesses, Homer then shows us not the hero's release but the world of Ithaca and the effect of Odysseus' absence on his wife and son. The need to find out about the fate of Odysseus leads to Telemakhos' journey to Pylos and Sparta in search of news and his own fame. Then Homer recapitulates the Olympian council and implements the freeing of Odysseus in Book Five. The effect is to suggest a double beginning and the simultaneity of Telemakhos' journey into the lands of his own maturity with Odysseus' voyage away from Kalypso through the great storm of rebirth that provides a fitting climax to Book Five.

What makes Kalypso so powerful and why does Odysseus spend such a long time with her? Such questions reach into the heart of both the epic and the hero. As has already been suggested, life in the Homeric world is subject to a natural ethic, the actual forces of existence and annihilation. For Homer existence is not merely given, for humans are mortal, but must be earned. In *The Odyssey* those who believe in life as mere ease lose themselves in heedless indulgence that is itself a form of death. Thus, we see in Odysseys' wanderings the omnipresent threat of the void that brings death through carelessness or forgetfulness. Hapless Elpenor suffers such a fate. He slept late on the roof of Circe's house the night before Odysseus had made the dreadful journey to the land of the dead. Odysseus relates Eplenor's untimely end this way:

> Waked by our morning voices, and the tramp
> of men below, he started up, but missed
> his footing on the long steep backward ladder
> and fell that height headlong. The blow smashed
> the nape cord, and his ghost fled to the dark. (BOOK 10, p. 184)[7]

Elpenor's death is the type of death in *The Odyssey*. Unlike the fierce confrontation of battle where mutual recognition of force and honor gives shape to both life and death in *The Iliad*, most of the deaths in *The Odyssey* occur through heedlessness. Even the clash of Odysseus and the suitors near the endof the epic presents death as the fate of the unwary:

> [Odysseus] drew to his fist the cruel head of an arrow for Antinoos
> just as the young man leaned to lift his beautiful drinking cup,
> embossed, two handled, golden: the cup was in his fingers:
> the wine was even at his lips: and did he dream of death?
> How could he?                    (BOOK 22, p. 409)

In *The Odyssey* death is not a glorious if painful epitome of life as it is for Hektor or even for Patroklos. In *The Odyssey* the herioc endeavor has lost its power to command belief, for death is now recognized as mere oblivion.

As George Dimock characterizes the ethic of the poem, *The Odyssey* has two primary stances: the stance of Odysseus, who gives and receives pain, and the stance of Kalypso, who cloaks and engulfs in forgetfulness. Dimock says, "Kalypso is oblivion. Her name suggests cover and concealment, or engulfing; she lives 'in the midst of the sea'--the middle of nowhere, as Hermes almost remarks--and the whole struggle of the fifth book, indeed of the whole poem, is not to be engulfed by the sea." Over against the power of cloaking forgetfulness and death stands Odysseus, whose name, Dimock suggests, means to give pain. Thus in *The Odyssey* "one must odysseus and be odysseused, or else be kalypsoed."[8]

The core of the first half of *The Odyssey*, the half that depicts the hero's absence from home and family, centers in the astonishing narration of the wanderings. This progression of stories about Odysseus' life after the Trojan war has exerted such a powerful hold on the imagination of readers that it seems not just the tale of one hero's adventures, but the pattern for all time of the quest for experience and dominance over the world. Stanley Kubric recognized this when he named his science fiction film *2001: A Space Odyssey*. The memorable events of the journey, the encounter with the giant Cyclops, the temptation of the sorceress Circe, the trip even to the land of the dead, reveal the heightened coloration both of adventure and of fantasy that strikes into the psyche of the audience. With remarkable suggestiveness Homer has these events appear not in the raw immediacy of the battle scenes in *The Iliad* but through the filtering and intesifying narration of Odysseus himself. Through his skill in story telling as in his guile at disguise Odysseus demonstrates that he is indeed *Odysseus polymetis*, "many-minded Odysseus."

Besides being adventures, the events of the great narrative are encounters with the natural ethic of the Homeric world. The outwitting of the Cyclops shows a brilliant but demented Odysseus, living out a version of fallacious immortality. His encounter with

Circe shows the powerful allure of the erotic and its dangers. And most importantly, the visit to the land of the dead confronts Odysseus with his personal and public mortality, his dead mother and the dead Achilles. Apparently for the first time, he learns from his mother his own vulnerability to death. His mother, Anticleia, tells him in one of the most moving passages in the poem:

> All mortals meet this judgement when they die.
> No flesh and bone are here, none bound by sinew,
> since the bright-hearted pyre consumed them down--
> the white bones long exanimate--to ash;
> dreamlike the soul flies, insubstantial.　(BOOK 11, p.192)

The visit to the dead is for Odysseus what the quarrel with Agamemnon became for Achilles, the harsh lesson of human weakness before impassive nature. The seven year long sojourn of Odysseus with Kalypso is like Achilles' sulk in his tent, both an escape from danger and a meditation on the problem of mortality. The meeting of son and dead mother shows the immediacy of death with unparalleled poignancy. Not only must Odysseus belatedly mourn his mother's death, but he learns that being the son of a mortal woman, he too must die.

The visit to the dead reveals personal vulnerability to death, but it also sheds new light on the public arena of the heroic endeavor. The Odysseus fresh from plundering "the stronghold on the proud height of Troy" betrays a harsh arrogance and egotism. The attack on the Kikones and the encounter with Polyphemos, the Kyklops, in Book Nine show an Odysseus all too secure in his role as conqueror. The fated journey to the land of the dead becomes Odysseus' dark night of the soul that continues until he is able to free himself from Kalypso. The crucial public episode in Hades is the meeting of Odysseus with his grand opposite Achilles. In Book Nine of *The Iliad* Achilles communicated his distrust of and perhaps distaste for Odysseus in rejecting both the Ithacan's speech on behalf of Agamemnon's bribes:

For as I detest the doorways of Death, I detest that man,
who hides one thing in his heart, and speaks forth another.
(*ILIAD* IX, ll. 312-13 )

In Hades Odysseus sees the haughty, proud Achilles still stung by
the ignominy of death and tries to soothe the great hero by flattery:
"was there ever a man more blest by fortune Than you, Achilleus?
Can there ever be?" With a harsh reply Achilles rebukes Odysseus'
arrogant belief in his ability to control any situation and then
renounces the entire heroic enterprise in doubt:

To this [Achilles] answered swiftly:
'Let me hear no smooth talk
of death from you, Odysseus, light of councils.
Better, I say, to break sod as a farm hand
for some poor country man, on iron rations,
than lord it over all the exhausted dead.' (BOOK 11, p. 207)

From the very mouth of Achilles at the heart of *The Odyssey* comes a
condemnation of the heroic ethic of honor that drives so many to death
in *The Iliad*. In *The Odyssey* the heroic project of war and honor has
been tarnished by grief and the realization of human limits. The only
way Achilles could have compensated for the death of Patroklos or for
his own dishonor would have been if he had attained immortality. But
even the great Achilles fell. Odysseus, now the greatest of living men,
finds himself in a world adumbrated by the shades of his mother and
Achilles. Odysseus' seven year stay with Kalypso is shadowed by his
experience and knowledge of the realm of death.

The second half of *The Odyssey* reveals directly the return of
Odysseus to his kingdom, to his own family, and to himself. The first
half of the epic shows the voyage out to the fabulous world of
adventure and toward psychic solitude. Now Homer presents the
gradual renewal of particular relationships and duties, the recovery of
social existence. When Aristotle calls *The Odyssey* a poem of *ethos*,
we usually interpret his word to mean 'character,' but we should also
consider character as the core of ethics in that a particular person

realizes himself in relationships and duties that are defining bonds of commitment, willing limitations on personal freedom. In this sense, *The Odyssey* explores the polarity between solitary being and social or ethical existence.

Homer dramatizes the process of the realization of Odysseus' character within an ethical context as a series of meetings, each one adding a new dimension to the man and his social nature. We see Odysseus in an astonishing sequences of meetings that reconstitutes the ethical world of relationsionships: meetings with his patron goddess, Athena, with his faithful swineherd, Eumaios, with his son, Telemachos, with the old servant woman, Eurycleia, with the suitors, with Penelope, with his father Laertes. In meeting, however, Odysseus does not reveal his identity immediately but hides in disguise, testing the truthfulness of the other person. Through most of this sequence he adopts the disguise of the beggar, image of man at the mercy of nature and gods. Odysseus' bitter experience of the dangerous world impels him to create testing situations--he has learned the descrepancy between appearance and actuality--but his recourse to disguise betrays a necessary uncertainty about his own identity and power. His belief in his own character was profoundly shaken by the visit to Hades and, as we have seen, in his seven year's detention from the world. The practical reason for his hiding in disguise is a need to ascertain the quality of feeling in his wife, son, and household, but in terms of action Odysseus finds himself physically up against terrible odds: one hundred and eight suitors against one hero, his son, and two faithful servants. The doubt about his physical strength and recognition, however, reflects an uncertainty in Odysseus about the validity of his own identity. Only by testing himself and others can the real Odysseus stand openly in the world of social existence.

The shift into a real world at the mid point of *The Odyssey* is masterfully portrayed by Homer. Odysseus returns, through the good graces of the Phaiakian navy, to Ithaca. He arrives asleep and wakes to see a still dream-like realm around him. When he learns that this is indeed Ithaca, the place becomes sensuously more concrete. While Odysseus has previously appeared to us largely through his own eyes and story in the first person narrative of the wanderings, he now is restored to a scene of Homeric realism where the poet views Odysseus with the same objectivity that he views all other characters. The effect of the arrival on Ithaca is one of focusing the attention of both hero and audience on the realitites of the world.

The first meeting in Ithaca, which establishes the mode of meeting for the rest of the poem, confronts the newly returned Odysseus with the disguised Athena. Strangely, but aptly, Odysseus, who has been transported home asleep by the Phaiakians, does not recognize his own island after twenty year's absence. Athena, disguised as a shepherd, must aquaint him with his own land. Simultaneously with his return to Ithaca, comes his reunion with Athena. Throughout the wanderings Athena has not been present to Odysseus, nor has she lent him any of her powerful assistance. In a sense, her absence from him is analogous to his absense from his own *ethos*. He has paid for the fabulous adventure into experience by a weakening of his own identity. Now at last the return of Odysseus to his native soil allows his reunion with his patron goddess, the immortal image of his own strength. More sure of his *ethos* now that he knows he is on Ithaca, he typically manipulates his identity and power through story telling.

> Odysseus, guarding himself, answered the disguised Athena,
>> with ready speech--not that he told her the truth,
>> but, just as she did, held back what he knew,
>> weighing within him at every step
>> what he made up to serve his turn.   (BOOK 13, p. 238)

The feint and conterfeint of goddess and hero both protect and reveal *ethos*--and the game of wits is an enjoyment for both. For Odysseus, the return to Ithaca and his reunion with Athena are essential parts of the process of restoring his identity. Because he is Odysseus again, giver and receiver of trouble, he is again the favorite of the goddess. The process of the realization of *ethos* is mutual. As Athena says,

> You play your part as if it were your own tough skin.
> No more of this, though. Two of a kind, we are,
> contrivers both. Of all men now alive
> you are the best in plots and story telling.
> My own fame is for wisdom among the gods--
> deceptions, too.                    (BOOK 13, p. 239)

The meeting between Odysseus and Athena sets the pattern for meeting from then on. Disguise, testing, revelation, and strengthening of identities proceed mutually throughout. Those met by Odysseus are forced through his deceptions and story telling to reveal themselves, tested by the wary hero. But he, too, is tested and forced to realize his own *ethos*, something far greater than the conqueror's egotism with which he began his journey from Troy. Mutual recognition, the exposing of true identity, continues until the very end of the poem.

The confrontation with the suitors provides both the dramatic climax of the poem and the attainment of public recognition that Odysseus needs if he is to rule again in Ithaca. The meeting with Achilles in the land of the dead yields its profit now, as Odysseus through cunning and strength is able to stave off death and claim his public identity in his homeland. Emotionally, however, the reunion with Penelope is the finest and deepest moment in *The Odyssey*. Just as the meeting with his mother showed Odysseus the finality of human life and the sterility of death, so the recognition and acceptance by the wary Penelope restores the hero to delight and human fertility.

The divorce between force and eros, between male and female energies so poignantly imaged in the fate of the wives of defeated heroes, after ten years of war and ten years of absence, can finally be overturned. The reunion of Odysseus and Penelope is the dramatic goal of *The Odyssey*, but it is also the thematic and psychological goal of Homer's protrayal of the entire heroic saga. The spectres of war and absence are finally dispelled in the pain and joy of husband and wife. Humanity and identity are now both recovered from the barren salt sea of existence.

> Now from his breast into his eyes the ache
> of longing mounted, and he wept at last,
> his dear wife, clear and faithful, in his arms,
> longed for
>     as the sunwarmed earth is longed for by a swimmer
> spent in rough water where his ship went down
> under Poseidon's blows, gale winds and tons of sea.
> Few men can keep alive through a big surf
> to crawl, clotted with brine, on kindly beaches
> in joy, in joy, knowing the abyss behind
> and so she too rejoiced, her gaze upon her husband,
> her white arms around him pressed as though forever.
> (BOOK 23, p. 436)

Looking back from the end of *The Odyssey* we can glimpse, however briefly, an Olympian view of Homer's world. *The Iliad* begins with the petition of a father for his captured daughter and ends with another father petitioning for the body of his dead son. The world at war shatters both the understanding between men and women and of the human family. Now in the end of *The Odyssey* we see the recovery of both eros and the family. The great Homeric epics, thus, have a cyclical realtionship that unites the powers of the masculine and the feminine and balances the terrors of war with the fruits of peace. Homer finds in humanity, in an Odysseus or an Achilles, in a Helen or a Penelope, a resilience and a beauty that remain breath-taking and inspiring after more than three thousand years. Not only is Homer our first poet, but he may be our best.

# Homer

## NOTES

[1] *The Iliad*, tr. Richmond Lattimore (Chicago: Univ. of Chicago Press, 1950). All quotations from *The Iliad*, save one, are taken from Lattimore's translation and are cited by book and line numbers from this edition.

[2] See "The Iliad, or the Poem of Force," tr. Mary McCarthy, first published in *Politics* (December 1945).

[3] Rachel Bespaloff, *On 'The Iliad'*, tr. Mary McCarthy (Princteon, N.J.: Univ. of Princeton Press, 1970), p. 48.

[4] This line, Book XXIV, l. 525-26, is taken from Rieu's translation because he captures in his prose at this point the more suggestive poignancy and poetry than does Lattimore. See *The Iliad* (Harmondsworth: Penguin, 1950), p. 451.

[5] See *The Poetics* (1459b).

[6] "The Name of Odysseus," *The Hudson Review* (Spring, 1956), pp. 52-70. The essay is readily available in George Steiner, *Homer: A Collection of Critical Essays* (Engelwood Cliffs, N.J.: Prentice-Hall, 1968).

[7] *The Odyssey*, tr. Robert Fitzgerald (New York: Anchor, 1962). All quotations from *The Odyssey* are from Fitzgerald's translation and are cited parenthetically by book and page numbers. Fitzgerald's translation does not follow Homer line by line as does Lattimore's, and thus line numbers are not so useful with Fitzgerald. It is a classicist convention to use Roman numerals for books from *The Iliad* and Arabic numerals when refering to books of *The Odyssey*.

[8] Dimock in Steiner, p. 145.

# Suggested Readings on Homer

The secondary literature on Homer is immense, not only because of the antiquity of the subject but because of the richness of the material. Homeric studies include scholarship on language, archeology, history, art, literature, philosophy, and many other fields. Here we indicate a few of the works and areas of Homeric study that are of interest to the informed beginning reader.

LITERARY CRITICISM:

Erich Auerbach, "Odysseus' Scar" in *Mimesis: The Study of Reality in Literature*, tr. Ralph Mannheim (Princeton, N.J.: Univ. of Princeton Press, 1953).

> Auebach's *Mimesis* is justifiably known as one of the most important works of modern literary criticism. Auerbach studies the relation between literary style and the concept of reality projected by a work. His chapter on Homer contrasts the Homeric presentation of clarity with the more mysterious and mystical presentation in the Bible. He contrasts the idea of a Homeric "foreground" with the Biblical use of "background."

Samuel Eliot Bassett, *The Poetry of Homer* (Univ. of California Press: Berkeley, 1938).

> Bassett was a classics scholar at the University of Vermont, and this book represents the proudest moment of the school's tradition of excellence in the Classics. Bassett shows a remarkable appreciation of the issues of poet and audience and of the artistic unity of the poems.

Rachel Bespaloff, *On 'The Iliad'* (Princeton Univ. Press: Princeton, N.J., 1948).

> Bespaloff's short book is unduly ignored these days. She presents as humane and immediate an appraisal of the tragic conditions of *The Iliad* as anyone. Her essays on Achilles, Hektor, and Helen are superb.

# Homer

George Dimock, Jr.,"The Name of Odysseus," *Hudson Review* (Spring, 1956), 52-70, reprinted in Steiner, below.

Dimock's essay is one of the classics of Homeric criticism. He explores the etymology of Odysseus' name and connects that to the basic ideas of the narrative.

*Homer: A Collection of Critical Essays*, ed. George Steiner (Prentice-Hall: Engelwood Cliffs, N.J., 1968).

Good introduction by Steiner along with a stimulating selections of essays including Auerbach's "Odysseus' Scar" and Kafka's parable of the Sirenes.

Simone Weil, "The Iliad, or the Poem of Force," tr. Mary McCarthy, first published in *Politics* (December 1945).

Weil's essay, written in the late 1930s, is shadowed by the spectre of the start of World War II. She emphasizes the dehumanizing power of war. Not exactly healthy reading, but impassioned and influential.

Cedric H. Whitman, *Homer and the Heroic Tradition* (Cambridge, Mass.: Harvard Univ. Press, 1958).

Whitman uses geometic art of the Dark Age of Greece as an analogue to the paterning of the Homeric poems, particularly *The Iliad*. Provocative work.

HOMER AND ARCHEOLOGY:

M. I. Finley, *The World of Odysseus*, rev. ed (New York: Viking, 1978).

Finley discusses the society, class, and economic structure of the Dark Age of Greece.

Jacquetta Hawkes, *The Dawn of the Gods* (New York: Random House, 1968).

This is a beautifully illustrated book and a good discussion of the culture and art of Homer's "Mycenae rich in gold."

William A. McDonald, *Progress into the Past: The Rediscovery of Mycenaean Civilization* (New York: Macmillan, 1967).

This is a helpful history of the development of archeology, particularly of the Mediterranean world. Important emphasis on Schliemann and his discovery of Troy and Mycenae.

THE HOMERIC QUESTION AND THE IDEA OF ORAL-FORMULAIC COMPOSITION:

G. S. Kirk, *The Songs of Homer* (Cambridge: Cambridge Univ. Press, 1962).

Kirk discusses the Homeric question at great length and explores those aspects of oral composition that help to explain some of the peculiarities of the poems. Kirk adheres to the theory of oral-formulaic composition of the Homeric epics.

A. J. B. Wace and F. H. Stubbings, *A Companion to Homer* (London: Macmillan, 1969).

This compendium of fairly recent scholarly understanding of the major topics concerning Homer is primarily intended for Classics scholars, but the summation of evidence on various aspects of the Homeric question and of the historical evidence is of general interest.

SOME TRANSLATIONS OF HOMER:

The tradition of Homer translations in English goes back to Chapman's version of the opening books of *The Iliad* in 1598. Shakespeare was influenced by this work in his play *Troilus and Cressida*. Other translations of note are by Dryden and Pope in verse; Butcher and Lang in prose. The best modern translations are by Richmond Lattimore and Robert Fitzgerald into poetry. Fitzgerald's *Odyssey*, in particular, is a masterpiece of translations. Lattimore's *Iliad* has been the stardard poetic version although Fitzgerald's more partisan, i.e., pacifist, translation is also well worth knowing. E. V. Rieu's Penguin versions of the two epics in prose are also quite accessible, even if the prose novelizes Homer just a bit too much. A particularly attractive edition is *The Illustrated Odyssey*, which uses the Rieu translation with many pictures of the geography of the Odyssian world as illustration

## Homer

(New York: A & W Publishers, 1980; there is a Penguin paperback of this edition available in England.)

Chapter Three

# THE PAIN OF LIMIT:
# THE TRAGIC VISION OF THE GREEKS

Along with the Homeric epics Greek tragedy has stood as the most important cultural achievement of the classical world. The tragedies of Aeschylus, Sophocles, and Euripides are not only the first extant plays in the Western tradition but also, at their best, the pinnacles of dramatic power, rivalled only by the finest plays of Shakespeare. The grandeur of the mythological material and the directness of presentation of character and story have inspired playwrights from Seneca to Racine to Sartre, and the idea of tragedy established in fifth century Athens has haunted the western imagination since before Aristotle analyzed the structure of tragedy descriptively in *The Poetics*, the most influential work of literary criticism. While the surviving version of *The Poetics* is admittedly terse, the essay provides the classic exposition of dramatic elements, such as plot, character, diction, thought, and melody. Aristotle's description of tragedy is familiar to most readers: tragedy is an imitation of an action in which a grand but flawed character suffers an unhappy reversal of fortune. What perennially appeals to readers and admirers of tragedy, however, has more to do with the content and experience of tragedy than with its structure.

Tragedy has an aura of mystery about it, for this form of drama stirs deep feelings and thoughts about the human condition that are represented by the plot and the characters. It is no accident that *Oedipus The King* by Sophocles became the root story of modern male psychology through the astute reading of Freud. When in the play

Iocaste, the wife of Oedipus, tries to assuage her husband's fears that he might marry his mother, she speaks to the strong relationship between dream, fantasy, and tragedy that Freud elaborated in his psychology:

> Have no more fear of sleeping with your mother;
> How many men, in dreams, have lain with their mothers!
> No reasonable man is troubled by such things.[1]

Iocaste at this time is, of course, still ignorant that her husband Oedipus is also her own son. But what she speaks illuminates a crucial aspect of the nature of tragedy. What we fear and avoid, trying to discount the lurking terror of our lives, becomes the very content of tragedy: extreme suffering, the transgression of primal taboos, excruciating guilt, and ultimately death. As Iocaste unwittingly comments, what we dream and pretend does not trouble us, but becomes the material of tragedy. Our nightmares and tragedy are fearfully close to one another.

The unavoidable truth of tragedy exposes suffering at the core of human nature. Without agony humans might come to believe that their external power and forms were absolute and sufficient, but tragedy opens the mysterious abysses of the primal world of the psyche. In tragedy, a man secure in his knowledge and power can only be a hollow man who must be destroyed so that his prouder, more disturbing yet truer self can emerge. Oedipus the powerful king is destroyed by knowledge. And yet, strangely, Oedipus gains in aura and wisdom from the terrifying suffering that comes from his knowledge. For many readers Oedipus is the type of the tragic protagonist, just as *Oedipus The King* was the type of tragedy for Aristotle.

The origins of Greek drama are obscure with only late reports and comments as our primary guides in place of early documents. The plays were associated with the Greater Dionysia, the Athenian spring festival in honor of the fertility god, Dionysus. By the middle of the

# The Tragic Vision of the Greeks

fifth century, plays were presented as trilogies of serious plays on mythic or heroic materials with a short satyr-play--usually a parody of the main trilogy--as comic relief at the end. Three sets of plays were presented on successive days before large audiences of townsmen, the priest of Dionysus, and the judges. Up to fifteen thousand spectators would attend the performances that were presented in a wooden amphitheater and later in the large marble theater that survives on the hill of the Acropolis. The sequences of plays were judged and prizes were awarded. According to surviving records, Aeschylus won first prize thirteen times during his lifetime, and Sophocles took first place fifteen times.

Drama in Athens apparently grew from choral odes or dythrambs in praise of the god Dionysus. According to legend, in about 537 B.C.E. Thespis became the first Greek to step forward as an independent voice and character, separate from chorus and chorus leader. In his honor to this day actors are called Thespians. In *The Poetics* Aristotle credits Aeschylus with the innovation of creating the second actor, which allowed dialogue to develop and plot to extend. In the same place Aristotle claims that Sophocles created the third actor's role and added scene painting to the spectacle of the drama. And indeed, Greek tragedy does use only three actors, who are given time to go behind the scene and change masks and costumes to emerge as new characters. In *Oedipus The King*, for instance, at the end of their quarrel Teiresias leaves the stage while Oedipus remains to confront his brother-in-law Kreon. With Oedipus and Kreon on stage the third actor changes costume to reenter a short while later in the persona of Iocaste. With the achievement of the three actors plus the chorus with its leader and with the introduction of scene painting the technical means of Greek theater were essentially completed.

For moderns the chorus is probably the strangest component of Greek drama. As drama changed, the chorus became less important, especially in the works of Euripides, but it was always part of the necessary means for tragedy. The chorus was composed in Sophocles' day of fifteen members, who would divide into two sub-choruses of seven each plus the leader. Especially in Aeschylus the chorus plays a dominant part. The odes of the Argive elders in the *Agamemnon* are among the most impressive passages in all drama as they reveal the dark and horrific past deeds of the house of Atreus and of early Greece. In *The Euminides*, the last play of *The Oresteia* trilogy, the ancient goddesses of blood revenge provide the title and become the chorus and focus of dramatic attention as Athena tries to forge a viable compromise between the powers of the Olympian gods and the energies of the earth goddesses. The dramatic effect of these choruses is tremendous. In performance the members of the choruses sang and danced their odes to a simple instrumental accompaniment and thus gave amplitude and spectacle to the production. The function of the chorus, as we now understand it, was not only to dramatize a community or group in the action but often to represent the audience of the play. Nietzsche in *The Birth Of Tragedy* explains the chorus in psychological and philosophical terms as representing the irrational and unconscious forces of human nature and the audience. For him the chorus is the soul of tragedy, existing as the mysterious central reality of human need and energy.

While the occasion and the means of Greek tragedy remained fairly constant, the variety of extant plays is astonishing. We have only about one-tenth of the dramatic production of the three great Athenian tragedians, but these surviving works constitute a dramatic achievement in range and depth that is equalled by no other single era. The sweep of Greek drama goes from the titanic struggles of Aeschylus to the psychological melodrama of Euripides. In general, although Euripides has the most surviving plays, seventeen in all, which shows his popularity in manuscript in later classical times, most readers have given the greater honor to Aeschylus and Sophocles. In his comedy on art and drama, *The Frogs*, Aristophanes shows a contest of artistic merit between Aeschylus and Euripides in which the older playwright wins hands down.

Aeschylus was the first of the three tragedians, and his plays show both a heroic breadth of vision and an expansiveness that are unequalled. The very theme of *Prometheus Bound*, the binding of the rebel titan Prometheus by the harsh god Zeus, is breathtaking, and Aeschylus' realization of the idea has stirred men's imaginations for twenty centuries. Such a play along with its thematic grandeur makes clear one of the prime elements of tragedy, *agon*, from which our word 'agony' comes. The Greek word means struggle and confrontation. While there is little overt action in *Prometheus Bound*, struggle of will and thought is everywhere present in it.

## I. *Prometheus Bound*:  Titan and Human

From the perspective of *The Poetics* of Aristotle, Aeschylus' play *Prometheus Bound* may be technically deficient in fulfilling the conditions of a tragic spectacle. At the same time, the reasons why Nietzsche considered Aeschylus to be the greatest of the tragedians, emerges from an understanding of the heart of the tragedy presented in *Prometheus Bound*. For Aeschylus is perhaps more nearly our contemporary in his understanding of pathos than he was of Aristotle. If there is a single image of Western man as recognizable in the ancient world as in the modern, it is that picture of the proud, defiant rebel Prometheus, chained and staked to a rock because he has arrogated to himself the power of divinity. In Greek mythology it is Prometheus who has given among other things the gift of fire to mankind and, thus, has contributed the most by any immortal to the definition of humanity.

In certain respects *Prometheus Bound* minimally satisfies Aristotle's requirements for a tragedy. There is a protagonist, Prometheus. There is an antagonist, Zeus. There is a plot, quite simple, with a beginning, a middle, and an end in view. There is a chorus which mediates the relation of the audience of the actors. The downfall of Prometheus is engendered by his hubris, the overstepping of the limits of his place in the cosmos. There is, however, no catharsis, no resolution where suffering brings purification for the chorus and is presented by Aeschylus as a hope for the protagonist.

The plot is already partially unfolded before the audience is introduced to the scene of Prometheus about to be chained with a stake through his heart to a rock in a place described as "the world's limit." Prometheus has foiled the intent of Zeus to rid the world of man--not man as we have come to know him, however, for man as we recognize him is presented as the creation of Prometheus. Before the intervention of Prometheus, the fate of mankind was pre-tragic and pre-historical. He was a creature of a day. He had neither sight nor craft nor medicine nor fire to warm himself. His condition was hopeless. He brooded incessantly over his coming death. Prometheus gave man hope, the instruments of power, the vehicle for remedying his failing fight with nature and, therefore, both his knowledge and autonomy. As was known to every spectator, the titan Prometheus was a demigod who could foresee the future till the end of time. His twin brother Epimetheus had the gift of recollection. He could know and measure the meaning of everything that had occurred in the past.

Prometheus has the power to rescue himself from punishment. Because of his foreknowledge he can guarantee his release by telling Zeus what union will bring his downfall. Obdurately, in the face of persecution and imprecations he refuses. Prometheus, it should be remembered, is deathless. His man-loving disposition comes from the bond he solidifies with mankind, but as one of the immortals. From a strictly logical standpoint, the action of the drama appears more like of a contradiction than a tragic paradox. If Prometheus has the gift of foreknowledge, then why does he engage in conduct that is sure to result in his torment?

# The Tragic Vision of the Greeks

Perhaps, Prometheus had only conditional foreknowledge; that is, if certain actions are undertaken, then certain effects follow. By refraining from causing these actions, the agent, then, will be spared the effects. In this way we might help to dissolve the dilemma by indicating that the kind of foreknowledge Prometheus has does not pertain to a world whose future has already been written in all its details. Fate, so understood, would depend upon freedom to transform a likely course of conduct.

A simple logical contradiction is transformed into a tragic paradox when the alternative resolutions are equally unacceptable. For Achilles the decision thrust upon him by nature was experienced as providing two mutually unacceptable and exclusive decisions. It was, therefore, inherently tragic. He had, in fact, two choices, each of which could be estimated to be inherently desirable. His tragic decision involves the denial of the recognition that the impossibility of incorporating both possibilities must lead to the annihilation of any future in order to realize an outcome which he cannot determine without foreknowledge.

From an existential perspective, *Prometheus Bound* is the most perfect tragedy conceivable. Unlike Oedipus, who unknowingly brings about his own downfall, and unlike any other protagonist in tragic drama, Prometheus is, from the outset, presented by Aeschylus as knowing and willing his own tragic condition. Prometheus is a hero without an unconscious. And, unlike Achilles, Prometheus is not plagued by mortality.

While later Sophoclean tragedy finds man as the offender and earlier Homeric tragedy presents an offenseless world, it is Aeschylus who elevates the human condition above the designs of nature. Prometheus is being overcome by sheer force, but will not yield in his conviction or stance. It is not accidental that it is 'might' who is personified by Aeschylus as ordering Prometheus to be bound. We cannot help but be sympathetic to a figure who has risked everything for man without benefit to himself. In Prometheus' opposition to a cruel and indifferent universe, Aeschylus makes room for authentic freedom of moral action and decision, which is at the heart of authentic tragedy. Man transcends the natural order, calling even the divinities to account in the name of purely human justice. Here is the first and most austere presentation of a humanism that defines religious existence within the realm of human understanding rather than taking man up into a divine drama.

The play centers on the meeting place of the foreknowledge, freedom, and fate of Prometheus. Prometheus suffers for the sake of justice freely willed. He is noble beyond dispute. He is courageous and through his awesome example gives heart to the wavering chorus, transforming them into figures worthy of their tragic predicament. Given the fact that Prometheus knows the outcome of his deed in advance of its happening, why does he complain of his wretchedness? Can it truthfully be said that Prometheus, endowed with foresight, was astonished at the consequences of his own doings? An insufficiency of foreknowledge calls into question again the degree of his understanding of the future. Yet, the province particular to Prometheus is knowledge of the future.

A real future is one that is radically contingent. It is not merely an eternally recurring image of the past. The density of time can be known in its fullness only as it is lived out. The future must be encountered and experienced before it can be said to be fully known. This is true of every creature of flesh for whom suffering can be predicated. It is neither in his divinity nor in his raw humanity that we, through the agency of the chorus, make the acquaintance of Prometheus, but rather in the midplace where a creature senses the divine possibilities inscribed in his sentient flesh. Prometheus complains as a mortal. He has linked himself inseparably to the fate of mortals. To know is to suffer the responsibility of knowing, that is, to know with care, to live as an embodied being.

# The Tragic Vision of the Greeks

All great tragedians have this much in common: the capacity to describe with precision experience as it comes upon us, not simply after the fact when all time is frozen and every moralistic judgement rendered irrelevant. Hence, the limits of advice can be marked only by one who, in the words of Prometheus, has one foot on the outside of calamity. The chorus cannot advise Promehteus as he would wish to be counselled because its heart beats differently from his own. Prometheus suffers because he is a being of flesh who authentically knows the future as it becomes present. Unlike Oedipus and every other tragic hero, he does not learn too late the insight necessary for right conduct. He knows what he has to do ahead of time. Still, he is capable of learning from the unfolding of existence, which is where all tragedy is rooted.

Aeschylus presents us with the purest tragedy imaginable from a philosophic viewpoint. It is yet more radical than Kierkegaard's description of the tragic cast of all philosophic understanding: "To live forward but to think backwards, this is the tragedy of thought." Still, it is tragedy with a tinge of resentment against all limitation. Authentic tragedy encompasses the knowledge of limitation, and yet, still suffers from an insufficiency, not of foresight, knowledge, or even existence. There is world enough and time, for Prometheus will live ten thousand years, long enough to witness his vindication. He suffers from living in a world indifferent to human complaint. He complains not so that Zeus will release him before his appointed time, for that is the way of treason, but rather to the chorus that they may become themselves as mortals.

## II. Aeschylus' *Oresteia*: A Communal Vision

Even grander than his treatment of the Prometheus is Aeschylus' presentation of the Agamemnon and Orestes story in *The Oresteia*. For here Aeschylus unfolded the long and tortuous journey of humans from brutal savagery to civilized existence. Where *Prometheus Bound* shows the story of the consequences of becoming human from the perspective of the eternal mountain top, *The Oresteia* presents the process of becoming human from within time and society--from the view of humans struggling toward the high city of justice and harmony.

Tragedies were presented in the early fifth century in trilogies of thematically related stories, and only later with Sophocles did the individual plays assume full independence with totally separate stories. Aeschylus' *Oresteia* stands as the only surviving complete trilogy of either sort, and in this we are immensely fortunate, for *The Oresteia* is the greatest conception in drama with only the Shakespeare history cycles and the Wagner *Ring* operas as possible rivals. Set against the Homeric epic of the Trojan war and its cruelty, *The Oresteia* traces the development of Greek civilization from its primitive roots through the bloody history of the family of Atreus, the father of Agamemnon and Menelaos. The central events of the three plays are revenge, murder, and the agonized search for the possibility of justice within history.

The three plays in the trilogy center on three crucial events, each forming a necessary stage in the evolution of a civilized polity: the murder of Agamemnon, the murder of Klytaimnestra, and the trial of Orestes. The *Agamemnon* builds to the brutal murder of the king by his wife Klytaimnestra and her lover Aigisthos in revenge for the blood sacrifice of the daughter Iphegeneia and for Atreus' grisly destruction of Thyestes' young children.

According to the dark legend behind the *Agamemnon*, the sacrifice of Iphegeneia, daughter of Agamemnon and Klytaimnestra, was needed to secure favorable winds for the embarkation of the Greek troops and ships against Troy. At an earlier time in the story, Atreus, Agamemnon's father, revenged himself for his wife's adultery with his brother Thyestes by murdering two of Thyestes' children and serving them in a horrible meal to their father. Aigisthos is the sole surviving child of Thyestes. Primitive rage reigns in the *Agamemnon* and bodies forth a savage world of hatred and blood revenge. Aeschylus suggests that the family of Agamemnon represents both Greek polity and Greek society in the chaotic period that followed the Trojan war. For moderns the characters also reveal powerful psychological forces that work both in the action and in the psyche. In particular we find the power of the outraged feminine and the quest of the children for maturity in the face of the terrifying parents.

In *The Oresteia* the great question emerges: how can a wrong be righted without merely entering into the circle of revenge? How, out of horror and savagery, can justice be secured? Orestes is the central figure of the trilogy, not because he is the most powerful or psychologically dominant character, but because he is the one who struggles to enact revenge ethically and consciously. In *The Libation Bearers*, the middle play of the trilogy, the exiled Orestes returns to Argos in disguise and murders his mother, Klytaimnestra, and Aigisthos. He has sought the advice of the god Apollo, who represents both the Olympian order of deities and the concept of reason. Under the advice of the god and striving to achieve revenge with justice, Orestes commits matricide. In keeping with his breadth of vision, Aeschylus sees both the ethical and the psychological implications of the great story, for his well intending Orestes does not rest secure in his deed but must be driven forth by the forces of primitive energies, the matriarchal earth goddesses of fertility and revenge, the Furies.

The final play in the trilogy, *The Eumenides* or in its more understandable translation, The Kindly Goddesses, raises the issue of murder to the level of theological and political theory. The central event of *The Eumenides* is the institution by Athena of trial by jury for the charge of murder. Orestes, haunted by the Furies, seeks refuge at the shrine of Athena in Athens on the Acropolis, the high city. After arguments by Apollo and by the Furies, the jury of citizens votes six to six in the matter of Orestes' guilt, but Athena breaks the tie by casting a vote for acquittal, siding as she says "with the father." The Furies, who represent not only blood revenge but the fertility of the earth as well, threaten to destroy Athens with plague and blight, but Athena promises these deities a shrine and sacred home in the city with a place of lasting honor among humans, and the Furies are appeased. They transform themselves and their energies into a blessing on the life of the city and become the Kindly Goddesses.

Aeschylus reveals through *The Oresteia* the rich meanings of the evolution of institutions and society as well as the strange blending in tragedy of suffering and joy. This trilogy is a cycle of civilization and of tragedy, initiating us into the broadest possible view of man and the communal need for tragedy. By the end of *The Eumenides* Aeschylus has dramatized the story of the Agamemnon family and how it led to the establishment of civic justice while also unfolding a tale of the psychological struggle of forces within individuals and society. Further, he develops the concept of tragedy from excruciating suffering in the murder of Agamemnon and Cassandra to the search for ethical action of Orestes' revenge to the detailing of the relation between personal suffering and communal renewal. Tragedy involves suffering and destruction , but it also suggests an essential movement toward regeneration. Aeschylus is notably explicit in *The Oresteia* in showing the affirmation in tragedy and in revealing the ultimate root of tragedy in the psychic life of the community. The fullness and implications of tragedy can best be found in the great *Oresteia* trilogy of Aeschylus.

## II.  Sophocles and the Tragedy of Character

With Sophocles tragedy became a more concentrated and detailed human process than it had been in Aeschylus or would be again until Shakespeare. Renouncing the idea of a thematic trilogy for the integrity of the single play, Sophocles wrote more than one hundred plays of which only seven have survived. The introduction of the third actor, an innovation even adopted by Aeschylus in his last works, allowed Sophocles to present more complex characters and a more varied kind of confrontation between them. In contrast with his great forerunner, Sophocles reduced the role of the chorus and placed the gods outside of the dramatic presentation, thus throwing a more sustained and greater attention on the individual struggles of his characters. Where Aeschylus portrays the *agon* of tragedy between men and gods or, as in *Prometheus Bound* between humanized titan and god, Sophocles presents the *agon* of human beings, each with a partial understanding of the truth of the gods and human fate.

Two of the greatest readers of tragedy, Aristotle and the German philosopher Hegel, found their prototypical tragedies in Sophocles' works. Each of these readers reveals his methodological bias but also lends great insight into Sophocles and tragedy in general. As has been mentioned, Freud, yet another profound mediator on tragedy and human fate, also found his model for psychic development in the drama of Sophocles.

Aristotle surpasses all later critics in his clarity of analysis and categorizing. In a way he deductively created the analytic categories of tragedy. His favorite tragedy is *Oedipus The King* because of the play's incisive presentation of situation and tragic fate and because of its structural lucidity. It is obvious that Aristotle particularly enjoyed the sudden reversals of fate and the wealth of recognition scenes in the play. (Sometimes in dramatic criticism these aspects of tragedy are referred to by their Greek names, such as *peripiteia* for reversal and *anagnorisis* for sudden recognition.) What pleased Aristotle in Sophocles still amazes the modern reader--the absolute structural control and clarity of the drama and the thrill of dread at the approaching moments of realization. More than any other playwright, Sophocles lays the action and its parts before the audience with complete directness and openness. In *Oedipus The King*, the masterpiece of dramatic construction, the first episode between the king and the blind prophet, Teiresias, shows the perfectly balanced conflict between authority in the day world of the polis and knowledge in the night world of the soul. What Aristotle does not comment on, but what surely must strike us, is the paradox of dramatic clarity and mysterious power in the play. While we, as audience, foreknow the catastrophe of the play, we also wince at every moment of Oedipus' self-ignorance. When as king of Thebes he swears to pursue the slayer of Laios as if the murdered king were his own father, we are ourselves made anxious at Oedipus' commission of parricide and at his frightening self-ignorance.

The nineteenth century German philosopher, Hegel, while not as popularly known as Aristotle, has contributed to our understanding in a remarkable series of writings on tragedy and its place in the esthetic and spiritual development of the West. Hegel was the great, if difficult, exponent of the evolution of consciousness in individuals and in nations and of the dialectical movement of thought. The German found his favorite play also in Sophocles, his choice being the *Antigone*, presents the idealism of Oedipus' daughter in the face of the tyrannical political claims of her uncle, Kreon. Against Kreon's ban on the burial of rebels against the state, Antigone carries out the ritual burial of her brother and is condemned to death. What Hegel sees as the core of tragedy is the conflict of ethical claims, the opposition of different ideas of ethics as embodied in particular characters.

> The principle source of opposition, which Sophocles in particular, in this respect following the lead of Aeschylus, has accepted and worked out in the finest way, is that of the body politic, the opposition, that is, between ethical life in its social univesality and the family as the natural grounds of moral relations.[2]

Sophocles' *Antigone* is the classic presentation of the ethical conflict between family and state, and we can see how this play would be particularly pleasing to Hegel. Antigone not only pursues the forbidden burial of her brother, Polyneices, but she further propounds publically the ethical stand that religious duty to family must take precedence over the claims of the state. Kreon, in complementary opposition, demands to be obeyed as the new king of Thebes and forbids the burial of all the slain enemies of the state, including Polyneices. Here Kreon champions and embodies an ethical commitment to the state that is in dialectical opposition to Antigone's position.

What Hegel helps to illuminate in Sophocles and in tragedy is the allegiance between individual drama and much broader categories of thought. For Hegel a tragedy is a passionate struggle of ideas in the process of defining conceptual truths about the human condition. While as moderns we may favor a more psychological emphasis on character, Hegel reminds us that thought and dialectical process are central to the meaning of tragedy.

### III. *Oedipus the King*: The Loneliness of Tragic Knowledge

> --The god dismissed my question without reply;
> He spoke of other things.

*Oedipus The King* is a play of riddles. In the legend and the play Oedipus lives his life and meets his fate through a web of riddling questions that he tries to overcome but to which he finally must submit. As an apparent stranger to the city of Thebes, years before the action of the play, he confronted the murderous Sphinx, herself the image of riddle, as Hegel says. She had presided over entry and exit to Thebes, asking her riddle and destroying each traveler who could not answer her rightly. The riddle was: what creature walks on four feet in morning, two feet at noon, and three feet at night? Oedipus solved the riddle and gave the right answer: that creature is man. In despair the Sphinx killed herself, and through his knowledge Oedipus became king over Thebes . Sophocles reveals through his play that the answer to the Sphinx's riddle may be man in general, but he shows us that Oedipus, in particular, as infant, man of power, and old man blinded by his own hand is the answer to the riddle. The Sphinx's riddle is about the nature of man and knowledge. Oedipus appears at the opening of the play in the noon of power and knowledge of the political world as he exerts his authority to solve the new plague that besets Thebes, a plague ominously reminiscent of the Sphinx's plague. But by the end of the action Oedipus has descended, as Shakespeare's Othello puts it, "into the vale of years."

Oedipus prides himself on his intellect, and the solving of the Sphinx's riddle has become the emblem of his knowledge. In the quarrel with the blind prophet Teiresias, Oedipus proudly contrasts his own knowledge in solving the riddle with the apparently useless knowledge of the old seer:

> Has your mystic mummery ever approached the truth?
> When the hellcat the Sphinx was performing here,
> What help were you to these people?
> Her magic was not for the first man who came along:
> It demanded a real exorcist. Your birds--
> What good were they? Or the gods, for that matter?
> But I came by,
> Oedipus, the simple man, who knows nothing--
> I thought it out for myself. (p. 20)

The answer to the Sphinx was literally "man," and Oedipus' solution was sufficient to avert that first plague, but the implications of the riddle are only brought to light by the entire action of the play.

Other riddles emerge in the play, both old and new. And rather than yielding definitive answers, solved riddles only produce new riddles. What is the cause of the plague, Oedipus enquires of Apollo at Delphi, and the oracle replies: Who is the murderer of Laios, for that murderer is a pollution in the city. Oedipus asks the prophet Teiresias, who killed Laios, and Teiresias replies: Who were your parents? A circle of riddling and questioning moves powerfully through the play with each apparent answer forcing the questioning to a more essential level. Just as Aeschylus weaves the family of Agamemnon into the

history of the evolution of civilization, so Sophocles weaves the figure
of Oedipus into the dramatization of the tragic nature of man. *Oedipus
The King* is about the nature of that creature who walks on four legs in
the morning, on two legs at noon, and on three legs at night. That
creature is Oedipus himself.

The core of the dramatic action centers on the parallel search for
the murderer of Laios and for the parents of Oedipus. The impetus to
alleviate the plague is deflected onto this double search by Teiresias'
posing of the question of identity:

> TEIR.: Your parents thought me sane enough.
> OED.: My parents again!--Wait: who were my parents?
> TEIR.: This day will give you a father and break your heart.
>
> (p.22)

In response to Oedipus' rash accusations, Teiresias has responded not
only with an accusation of Oedipus, but with the posing of the Sphinx's
riddle in a new form. If Oedipus is such a genius at solving riddles,
does he know who his own parents are? Of course the issue of
Oedipus' parentage is wrapped in obscurity both in his own
consciousness and in the cruel actions of his parents. Behind both the
motivation of the parents and of Oedipus himself lies the fearful oracle
of Apollo.

As Oedipus recounts in his first long scene with Iocaste, his
relation to Merope and Polybus of Corinth, his supposed parents, was
shaken by the rebuke of a drunken man at a banquet long age: (he)
"cries out that I am not my father's son" (p.40). In anguish over his
parentage Oedipus seeks out the oracle of Apollo, but instead of a clear
answer he receives the riddle of his fate:

> The god dismissed my question without reply;
> He spoke of other things. Some were clear,
> Full of wretchedness, dreadful, unbearable:
> As that I should lie with my own mother, breed
> Children from who all men would turn their eyes;
> And that I should be my father's murderer. (p.41)

Horror at doing such things drove Oedipus to abandon his ties to Corinth, and on the road to Thebes he met a harsh old man and his retainers at the crossroad: "I killed him. I killed them all."

A little earlier Iocaste had told of the unreliability of the oracle, citing the prophecy that Laios would be killed by his own son. Iocaste and Laios forestalled the oracle by having the infant's feet pinned and by placing the child on the Kithairon mountain to die. The audience knew and Teiresias knew and we as readers know that the infant was Oedipus and that he has killed his father and married his mother. We are tempted to draw back from the story to castigate Oedipus for not learning with certainty about his parentage and for ever killing or marrying anyone. But the issues of Oedipus' volition and previous actions are not at the heart of the play. There is never any question from Apollo's point of view that Oedipus can only be Oedipus by killing his father and marrying his mother. Similarly, the answer to the riddle of the Sphinx is that Oedipus is man bound by nature in infancy, maturity, and old age. Oedipus in the play is the man who crawls, walks, and hobbles, who kills his father and marries his mother. The oracle has already been fulfilled and the riddle solved before the opening of the play. *Oedipus The King* is not about action but about knowing and suffering the truth.

Who is Oedipus? At the opening of the play he appears in royal robes with the staff of kingly power in his hand. He is the man who knows the world because he has solved the Sphinx's riddle. But of course he does not know the implications of his answer; he does not know in what way he was an infant nor in what way he will be an old man, but suffering will teach him. The god will not let Oedipus only be the man who killed his father and married his mother; Oedipus must come to know what he has done and to suffer who he is. In this Aristotle was profoundly right; *Oedipus The King* is the great play of reversal and recognition. Courageous before the horror of his own fate, Oedipus must know. The Theban shepherd, against his will, is compelled to reveal who the infant on Kithairon was:

> SHEP.: Ah, I am on the brink of dreadful speech!
> OED.: And I of dreadful hearing. Yet I must hear. (p.61).

In a flood of recognition that is suffering and knowing together, Oedipus rushes into his palace.

Who is Oedipus? At the end of the play he is a beggar, self-blinded, leaning on the staff of bodily weakness. He is the man who knows because he has suffered to be at one with his terrifying identity.

> Apollo. Apollo. Dear
> Children, the god was Apollo.
> He brought my sick, sick fate upon me.
> But the blinding hand was my own!
> How could I bear to see
> When all my sight was horror everywhere? (p. 70).

Fate was given by Apollo, but human suffering was effected by Oedipus. Now in the image of mysterious knowledge, the blind old man, the new Teiresias, Oedipus gains a stature and a fullness beyond even our safe knowledge. He has journeyed into a land where he can know and suffer and be the limit of what is man: "Of all men, I alone can bear this guilt" (p. 72). Who is Oedipus? He is the man who has killed his father and married his mother, He is the creature that walks on four legs in the morning, on two legs at noon, and on three legs at night.

## IV. Epic, Tragedy, Philosophy

What Hegel helps to illuminate in Sophocles and in tragedy, generally, is the allegiance between individual drama and philosophic categories of thought. For Hegel a tragedy is a passionate struggle of ideas in the process of defining conceptual truths about the human condition. While as moderns we may favor the more psychological emphasis on character, Hegel reminds us that thought and the and the dialectical process are central to the meaning of tragedy. Through Hegel's commentaries on tragedy, we begin to glimpse the emerging continuum of Western culture in its beginnings, from the epic confrontations of Homer to the dialectical oppositions of tragedy and then toward Platonic dialogue and Aristotelian analysis. It is this unfolding continuum that we are pursuing in our discussion of the Greek roots of our cultural and intellectual tradition.

Nietzsche in *The Birth of Tragedy* presents a characteristically provocative interpretation in his discussion of tragedy as the most life affirming of cultural forms. For Nietzsche tragedy only superficially deals with a pesimistic sense of existence. The hero who is destroyed is, in this view, the sculptural figure, representing the conscious aspects of human nature. In Nietzsche's terminology, the tragic hero partakes of the Apollonian mode. The core of tragedy, here, is not the tragic protagonist but the chorus, which embodies the unconscious energies of human existence, outwardly mourning for the fall of the hero, but in essence jubilant in the intensity that liberates the most profound energies of human existence. Here Nietzsche finds the triumph of the Dionysian.

Hegel and Nietzsche, as well as Aristotle, show us the seriousness of tragedy both as cultural experience and as a crucial revelation of human thought and meaning. If we take a long view of the relation of epic and tragedy, we see a fierce duality of character and situation that intensifies both drama and thought. The great meetings of Priam and Achilles, of Odysseus and Penelope, of Oedipus and Teiresias, contain contain some of the most moving scenes in all of literature, but they also embody the stucture of thought. Plato, although sceptical of the role of the poets in his *Republic*, surely learned the essence of thinking and the pursuit of truth from Homer and the tragedians. While Plato makes the turn toward reason that led to a great division within human knowledge, he preserves an integrated sense of person, speech, and thought in his dialgoues. In response to Achilles, Odysseus, and

## The Tragic Vision of the Greeks

Oedipus, Plato celebrates the living embodiment of philosophy and its project, Socrates.

## NOTES

1*Oedipus the King* in Sophocles, *The Oedipus Cycle*, tr. Dudley Fitts and Robert Fitzgerald (New York: HarBrace, 1969), p. 49. Quotations from *Oedipus the King* are from this edition and are cited by page number.

2*Hegel On Tragedy*, ed. Anne and Henry Paolucci (New York: Harper, 1975), p.68.

# Suggested Readings on Tragedy

GENERAL CRITICISM AND BACKGROUND ON GREEK TRAGEDY:

Aristotle, *The Poetics* (many translations and editions).

> The first and most influential of all literary criticism. Any student of Greek drama must be acquainted with Aristotle's structural definitions of tragedy, its elements, the tragic hero, and the idea of the tragic flaw. Essential, if dry, reading.

Peter Arnott, *An Introduction to Greek Tragedy* (New York: St. Martin's, 1959).

> Arnott's book surveys the history and dramaturgy of the ancient Greeks for the general reader. Helpful basic material on Greek drama and dramatists.

G. W. F. Hegel, *Hegel On Tragedy*, ed. Anne and Henry Paolucci (New York: Harper and Row, 1975).

> The reflections of the German idealistic philosopher on tragedy are important, if difficult. Hegel emphasizes both the ethical conflicts in tragedy, and the dialectical opposition of characters and issues.

H. D. F. Kitto, *Greek Tragedy* (London: Methuen, 1966).

> Kitto represents the mainstream of English scholarship and criticism for the beginning reader. Good discussions of the three major tragedians and their plays.

Jan Kott, *The Eating of the Gods: An Interpretation of Greek Tragedy*, tr. Boleslaw Taborski (New York: Random House, 1973).

> Kott is an existentialist, who experienced the dark days of World War II in Poland. He is definitely not a standard critic, but a very provocative one. He blends philosophical, political, and anthropological approaches to Greek drama. Definitely worth a look.

Friederich Nietzsche, *The Birth of Tragedy out of the Spirit of Music* and *The Case of Wagner* , tr. Walter Kaufmann (New York: Vintage, 1967).

> *The Birth of Tragedy*, Nietzsche's first major work, addresses the fundamental tensions between the rational and the irrational dimensions of human nature as experienced in tragedy. The work was partly inspired by the German opera composer Wagner's opera*Tristan and Isolde*, and it includes, besides certain reflections on opera and tragedy, the first of Nietzsche's attacks on the rationalism of Plato and especially Socrates. Difficult but ultimately fascinating material.

WORKS ON SPECIFIC DRAMATISTS:

ON AESCHYLUS:

Aeschylus, *The Oresteia*, tr. Robert Fagles, commentary by W. B. Stanford (New York: Viking, 1975; Penguin, 1984).

> Along with a good translation of the whole *Oresteia*, this edition provides a long and detailed interpretive essay by Standford as well as a substantial section of explanatory notes.

*Aeschylus: A Collection of Critical Essays*, ed. March H. McCall, Jr. (Englewood Cliffs, N.J.: Prentice-Hall, 1972).

> A helpful selection of essay by different hands on various plays of Aeschylus.

Brooks Otis, *Cosmos and Tragedy: An Essay on the Meaning of Tragedy*, ed. Knopf ( Chapel Hill: Univ. of North Carolina Press, 1981.)

> Otis was one of America's finest classics scholars; he was famous for his work on Virgil. Here he explores *The Oresteia* and Aeschylus' attempt to transcend the mode of tragedy.

George Thompson, *Aeschylus and Athens* (London, 1966).

> Thompson investigates the connections between Aeschylean tragedy and the social, political, and religious contexts of Athens. Detailed; interesting for the connection of literature and history.

## The Tragic Vision of the Greeks

ON ARISTOPHANES (included for a complement to tragedy and for reference to the Plato chapter):

Aristophanes, *The Clouds, The Frogs*, tr. Dudley Fitts in *Four Plays by Aristophanes* (New York: Harcourt, 1970).

> Good, accessible, understandable translations of Aristophanes are hard to come by. Fitts's are among the best. *The Clouds* shows Aristophanes' view of Socrates; *The Frogs* shows a view of the art of drama and the status of the tragic poets.

K. J. Dover, *Aristophanic Comedy* (Berkeley: Univ. of California Press, 1972).

> A helpful introduction to Aristophanes with sections on the theater, performance, and comment on each play.

Leo Strauss, *Socrates and Aristophanes* (New York: Basic Books, 1966).

> A famous, conseravtive political philsopher discusses the conflict between Aristophanes' commitment to a healthy society and his distrust of the philosophical stance of Socrates.

ON SOPHOCLES:

C. M. Bowra, *Sophoclean Tragedy* (Oxford: Oxford Univ. Press, 1944).

> A classic commentary on the plays of Sophocles.

Cedric H. Whitman, *Sophocles: A Study of Heroic Humanism* (Cambridge, Mass.:Harvard Univ. Press, 1951).

Chapter Four

# THE TURN TOWARD REASON:
# SOCRATES AT THE VORTEX OF WORLD HISTORY

Socrates lived from 469 to 399 B.C.E. It is Socrates, whom Nietzsche, the greatest modern student of the ancient Greeks, called "that great vortex and turning point in world history." The first stirrings of philosophy pre-date Socrates. But the impact of Socrates is evident from the fact that philosophic figures who come before Socrates are referred to till our own day as "Pre-Socratics."

The various ways that the birth of reason pre-dates the life of Socrates must be understood if we are to recognize the context in which the thought of Socrates emerges, and perhaps more significantly, where the thought of Socrates is taking us. For the Homeric world, the deepening sense of tragedy, and the history of Athens provide indispensible clues to our appreciation of the Socratic enterprise. Since Socrates himself wrote down nothing at all (it is even said of him by Plato that Socrates regarded the alphabet with a certain suspicion), we must first recognize our sources for understanding Socratic philosophy.

In this respect, we have been helped immeasurably by contemporary scholarship. The art of reading a Platonic dialogue is one of the major accomplishments of twentieth century philosophic investigation. This is of great importance because it is the dialogues of Plato that provide us with the thinker whom we today recognize as the formative figure in the history of philosophy.

Plato, the student of Socrates lived from from 427 to 347 B.C.E. It is to the student of Plato, Aristotle, that we first look in order to grasp the most widely held vision of Socrates' work. Aristotle studied in the Academy of Plato from the time he was 18 years old until he was 36. He could never have met Socrates, since Plato himself was but a young man in his late twenties when Socrates was condemned to death by the Athenian democracy. Aristotle states that Socrates contributed to the advancing of philosophy in three fundamental respects. In the first place, Socrates focused on matters of right conduct, or what we now call ethics. In the second place, according to Aristotle, Socrates was concerned with what is essentially the same in all changing circumstances. These eternal truths were only subsequently elaborated by Plato, and thus, according to Aristotle, it was Plato who put into the mouth of Socrates Plato's own theory of forms. Thirdly, Aristotle states that Socrates was involved in a new method for advancing philosophic study. What we today call the "Socratic method" involves a disciplined form of asking and answering questions. The essence of this new form of enquiry is "dialectical" thinking.[1]

We see dialectical thinking at work in the way in which Socrates is presented in a Platonic dialogue. While the content of the subject investigated changes, the form of argument remains the same in its essential aspects. Socrates asks his interlocutor (the one with whom he speaks) *to ti*, what is it? In the *Laches*, "*to ti*" refers to courage. The essential question of the *Laches*, then, is "what is courage?" In the *Lysis*, the fundamental question is "what is friendship?" In the *Meno*, the essential question is "what is excellence?" The ancillary question of the *Meno* is: "Can virtue be taught?" In general the dialogues are named after the interlocutor. Such is the case with the *Euthyphro*, whose essential argument we shall reconstruct.

The phenomenon of Platonic-Socratic dialectic begins with the asking of the *to ti* question. In the case of the *Euthyphro*, the question is: "What is holiness?" From a strictly dialectical standpoint, the question develops out of a commonly held opinion (in Greek, *homologia*). The prevailing opinion is accounted as possessing at least a kernel of understanding. Guiding this assumption is the view that a shared, collective opinion carries a certain degree of power or influence over the polis (the body politic) and is, therefore, a force to be reckoned with. However, an opinion is not necessarily a "right opinion." It needs to be scrutinized, clarified, and made answerable before the court of reason.

This process is advanced by raising the level of discourse from commonly or casually held opinion by sharp questioning concerning the origins and consequences of holding to such an opinion. Once challenged the opinion is purified of what is manifestly deficient in holding to it. The *homologia* then moves from the realm of prejudice, custom, and personally privileged position to the realm of *logos* or reason. Socrates asks for reasons for holding to the original position. In essence Socrates is asking the interlocutor to justify his statements in the face of rigorous interrogation. A shared discourse, the joint pursuit of just reasons for arriving at a satisfactory position, is the objective of the philosophic quest.

The original opinion is expanded by a movement of deleting what is unjustifiable and preserving what appears to be true. Socrates explains that what he wants is not merely an opinion but a right opinion that he can hold together with his interlocutor. Together, Socrates and the interlocutor, are searching for that which is unchanging in all changing circumstances, to recall the comment of Aristotle. Socrates moves from the looks of things to an inherent reality. The reflection of this inherent reality is an *eidos*, or as it reads in Latin, an "idea." The idea must match certain preconceived, although most often unstated, criteria.

The form of the idea takes a certain methodological precedence over the content of the idea. An *eidos* is universal in its reach. This means that it must be binding on all persons, at all times, in all places. Otherwise, a change in time, location, or disposition would be permitted to diminish the compass of the idea. Each alteration in circumstance would lead to confusion, anxiety, and uncertainty. Moreover, the political implications would lead to instability where power would measure knowledge and force would rule understanding. This is another way of saying that the *homologia* would be accepted as each society conceived it. What is true of courage, friendship, justice, or holiness could differ from Athens to Sparta. By definition, we would then lose what is true for all, that is, what is universal.

The engine that fires Platonic-Socratic dialectic along is the principle of non-contradiction. The principle of non-contradiction holds that a thing cannot both be and not be in the same place, in the same respect, at the same time. The word "contradiction" derives from the Latin root word "to speak" and the prefix "contra," meaning against. A logical contradiction involves asserting that something both is and is not the case, in the same place, at the same time, and in the same manner. In a Platonic dialogue it is the recognition of a contradiction that is crucial. For a contradiction cannot stand still. It must be overcome. Thus, the recognition of a logical contradiction is decisive in forcing a move in the argument to a higher level where the contradiction is dissolved, resolved, or incorporated into an ongoing stage with the argument awaiting later resolution.

There is a special kind of contradiction which is unique to a Platonic dialogue in Greek philosophic thought. When a speaker's actions belie his words, then he is involved in contradiction that moves beyond the realm of statements colliding with each other. To assert what one has denied or to deny what one has asserted is to enter into an existential contradiction. The speaker's own existence, the discrepancy between what he says and what he does, involve him in an "existential contradiction." For Socrates to praise courage, while displaying cowardice, would evidence an existential contradiction. Here, Plato through his presentation of the figure of Socrates, assures the reader of the existential consistency of Socrates. To know what justice is means acting in a just way. Socrates is described in an epilogue to his death as the "wisest, most just, and best man of our times." Very often, Socrates reveals to his interlocutor that his statements are belied by his actions. Such is the case with Meletus and Anytus, the accusers of Socrates in the *Apology*. Socrates is charged with corrupting the youth of Athens as well as with impiety. In his defense Socrates notes that his accusers spend no time at all with the youth of Athens. How, then, can they maintain that they care for them, or are genuinely concerned with their ethical conduct? The actions of his accusers reveal a fundamental existential contradiction. The concept of existential contradiction takes us beyond the realm of pure logic into the domain of psychology.

Originally, the study of the psyche was focused upon the soul. It is the psyche of persons that Socrates is above all concerned with educating. One must first begin with awakening an individual to what remains concealed to him about his own psyche. In the Platonic dialogues Socrates is concerned with educating the whole person. To do so means, inescapably, calling attention to inertial self-forgetfulness. To think involves thoughtfulness that brings the recognition that dialectical argument begins and ends with the self, cognizant of the intimate relation of speech to deed.

The project of Platonic-Socratic dialectic involves a transforming of the complete psyche. The psyche is itself divided into three recognizable aspects. The most encompassing of the three aspects of the soul is eros, meaning love or desire.[2] As a careful reconstruction of the *Symposium* shows eros is defined by the subject to which it attaches itself. All human action and reflection are, for the Platonic Socrates, erotically charged. Education which leaves the realm of eros untouched is not education in any serious sense for Socrates. Where one's desire is, there also, we shall find the intentions of the psyche. To educate means to draw eros away from the sources of immediate gratification toward the the enduring satisfaction that comes from knowing the intelligible forms of enduring beauty (*Republic* 437-441;

*Phaedrus* 246 ff.).[3] Eros does not emerge in a vacuum. The psyche, on the Socratic-Platonic model, is intimately bound up with the reflected sense of self that occurs in the reactions of others with whom we live. *Thumos* is the spirited element by which we experience pride and shame within the psyche. When it acts moderately, *thumos* binds the psyche to *logos*. It performs the dual function of forcing eros to postpone its desire for immediate gratification while at the same time returning *logos* to the subject in a manner that resists the depersonalizing of reason. *Thumos* is, therefore, the source of self-respect and ethical responsibility that elevates the human psyche to the sphere of shared civic and political life.

To love that which is truly worthy of our love, to honor that which deserves to be called honorable, it is necessary to know what is good. Otherwise, in the name of love one can cause harm rather than benefit, and in the name of honor, engender tyranny or chaos rather than proper honor. It is only philosophy which provides instruction about reality which reflects the knowable order of things. The manifold objects of sensory impression are first registered imagistically, or in the Greek, as *eikasia*. An image is vivid and awakens what is latent in sensory apprehension. The stability of a wavering image is fixed by turning the images of an object toward the objects imaged or imitated. The poet, whom Socrates interrogates in the *Apology* deals primarily in the creative apprehension and use of images. When asked for an explanation of his own artistry, he is not necessarily able to interpret the sources of his inspiration, and it is in this sense that he is said to be lacking in wisdom or in Greek, *sophia*.

Similarly, the craftsman deals with the manipulation of objects, forging their configuration so as to make such objects of practical use. Without the fire of human invention, the gift of Prometheus to mortals, human beings would be incapable of mere survival. All the arts and crafts responsible for what we call civilization, Plato characterizes as *techne* an essential but not exhaustive form of

82

knowledge. When Socrates, in the *Apology*, interrogates the craftsmen regarding the nature of wisdom, he discovers that, while they understand their particular craft, they are unable to answer what wisdom is in itself. For wisdom, *sophia*, is necessarily concerned with value and meaning. It extends beyond the realm of utility characterized by *techne*. As John Wild puts it: "In fact, it is through knowledge alone that man has any access to other values,for we cannot even strive to do a good we do not know. Hence the greatest force and power is useless to us and becomes harmful if we do not know how to use it."[4] In the realm of *techne*, there is a generalized intention toward the progression of making our suppositions about how things work more useful. As Socrates makes clear in the *Euthyphro*, it is not the kind of of knowing that provokes enmity:

> SOCRATES: Was it not also stated, Euthyphro, that the gods revolt and differ with each other, and that hatreds come between them?
>
> EUTHYPHRO: That was stated.
>
> SOCRATES: Hatred and wrath, my friend--what kind of disagreement will produce them? Look at the matter thus. If you and I were to differ about numbers, which of two was the greater, would a disagreement about that makes us angry with each other and make enemies of us? Should we not settle things by calculation, and so come to an agreement quickly on any point like that?
>
> EUTHYPHRO: Yes, certainly. (*Euthyphro* 7b,c) [5]

Calculation and measurement produce accord and uncover order in things. However, the end at which the ordering of thought aims remains to be established. It is at this critical juncture that the wisdom of the ancients begins to be differentiated from that of the moderns.

Thinking in an orderly way depends, for Plato, upon a grasp of intelligible objects that are independent of sensory apprehension, in Greek, *epithumia*. The division between intelligible and sensory objects mirrors the division between mind and body (psyche and *soma*). Such thinking, which first concerns itself with the realm of intelligible objects, is called by Plato *dianoia* and is inseparably connected with mathematics. Here, we enter the realm of reality antecedent to the way things just look, that is, the domain of appearance. Thinking on the verge of discovery--the constants ordering their own movements--is the central task of dialectic. Pure numbers (*arithmos*) and the apprehension belong to the theoretical enterprise of Greek mathematics and emerge from two primary practical activities, counting and calculating. The action of counting supposes that there are pure, i.e., indivisible numbers, that are able to be counted off. Calculating refers to the act of relating numbers to one another. Such pure numbers can be grasped only through thought,and are in themselves, uniform and indivisible units.

The relation of matter to form is intimately tied to Plato's theory of mathematics. The concept of organizing thought into concrete patterns necessitates both an understanding of the role of counting and the work of calculating. The problem of the possibility of such assemblages, i.e., the question how it is possible that many "ones" should ever form one collection of "ones," leads to the search for *eide* with definite "specific properties" such as will give unity to,and permit a classification of, all counted collections. Greek arithmetic is therefore originally nothing but the theory of the *eide* of numbers.[6]

The material (*hyle*) content of such *eide* is recognized through the inductive process of calculating the phenomena to be formed. For the Greeks this is called "theoretical logistics." In Plato these pure units have an independent being of their own and through the general process of *dianoia* make it possible to conceptualize the world in an organized fashion.

From out of the realm of the indefinite (*apeiron*) emerges the distinct, the definite, and the determined attributes of any given subject. The ultimate unity of all being is dialectically arrived at through division (*diaresis*) which makes thought possible and tasks manageable. It is in this swirl of the multiplicity of everyday existence that life is lived out. Hence, it is necessary that a Platonic dialogue image everyday discourse. The dramatic unity and form of the dialogues are drawn from the diverse materials and figures of everyday life in Athens. Reading a Platonic dialogue involves an appreciation of the action of the drama that binds deed and speech together.

## I. Reading A Platonic Dialogue: The *Euthyphro*

Reading a Platonic Dialogue involves an appreciation of its intimate intertwining of drama, thought, and form. There are certain recurrent patterns that give shape to Socratic inquiry as presented by Plato in the form of the dialogue. Almost none of the dialogues are lectures or orations where Plato unequivocally offers a set of propositions, axioms, or even philosophic positions to the reader in a direct fashion. This method of indirection or process presents the formidable challenge to the reader of determining the view which Plato holds to be true and certain on any given subject. It is usually, but not always the case, that the words of Socrates reflect Plato's own position. Because Socrates is more apt to ask a question than to answer one, a further challenge is presented to the reader in trying to determine what Socrates means as opposed to what he says. The indirection of presentation assumes a wakeful patience that may be lacking for the interlocutor--the person to whom Socrates is speaking, and after whom the dialogues are most often named--but a patience that must be cultivated by the active reader.

Unlike the expositions of Aristotle which tend to dwell on separate domains of investigation, the Platonic dialogue is harder to specify in terms of its precise content. The various branches of philosophy have not yet been divided into sub-disciplines which make analysis of component parts more accessible. While Aristotle treats ethics, metaphysics, logic, psychology, politics, and poetics as distinct subjects, the Platonic dialogue remains much closer to our immediate experience of the world where everyday events are mixed up with questions about ultimate reality, and very often fatigued by daily happenings and obligations. When Socrates claims that he is not a teacher in the strict sense, he positions himself on the side of that view of philosophy which is democratic, open, and self-critical. Here every aim is taken from the position of learner as well as teacher, the moments alternating with perspective but united before the common court of human reason.

The *Euthyphro* opens with dramatic irony as Socrates and his interlocutor stand before the portals of the (civil) court. For, this is, as Euthyphro remarks, not one of the places Socrates is accustomed to haunt. The trial of Socrates on the charge of impiety awaits him in the scene framed by the discourse with Euthyphro on the nature of holiness. Euthyphro is at court, Socrates learns, to prosecute his own father for having unintentionally murdered one of his slaves. The father had found another slave killed by the first slave and not knowing what to do, placed him bound as a hostage in a ditch until his return with an answer from a religious authority. In the meanwhile the slave died. What does one do when there is no authority nearby and a person must go in search of one? In the case of the slave who perished from the lapse of time, this death-dealing delay was thought by Euthyphro, who is a self-taught theologian, to have been an act of wanton murder and therefore an expression of impiety.

With irony Socrates asks Euthyphro, a self-claimed expert on the gods, whether he is willing to take Socrates as his student. Socrates says that he will then be able to better answer the charges brought against him by the poet Meletus and others who have accused him of impiety. For surely any man who freely takes his own father to court in a capital case must be secure in his knowledge of what is pleasing to divinity. In the realm of lived-time Socrates suppresses any anxiety that he might have about his impending trial and engages the unknowing Euthyphro in a classical example of the Socratic method of inquiry. The dramatic indications given by Plato at the beginning of the dialogue already indicate the price to be paid for trying to escape the task of philosophy. Reasoning takes time, yet is capable of saving lives. The father of Euthyphro, had he been his own authority, would not have suffered a death-dealing delay that brought about the present predicament.

The inital task of philosophy was revealed to Socrates, as he tells us in the *Apology*, during a visit to Apollo's temple at Delphi. To "know oneself," *gnothi seauton*, is the inscription that Socrates saw upon the doorposts of the temple. There is a two-fold charge implied in these words: to know one's self means to have self-knowledge and this in turn means that the dialogical process of thinking aloud in the presence of another can become second nature when it is interiorized. A Platonic dialogue properly approached and appreciated is no less than the dramatization of thought coming upon itself and is therefore a demonstration in the task of human liberation where reasoning is synonymous with genuine autonomy. Socrates asks for reasons for everything even in places we should not expect it.

Euthyphro cannot permit the father-son relation to stand in the way of acting piously. Although other men may scorn him for his conduct, Euthyphro brings precedent as a kind of proof for his actions:

> And these same men admit that Zeus shackled his own father [Cronos] for swallowing his [other] sons unjustly, and that Cronos in turn had gelded his father [Uranus] for like reasons. But now they are enraged at me when I proceed against my father for wrong doing, and so they contradict themselves in what they say about the gods and what they say of me. (*Euthyphro* 6a)

Euthyphro has more than precedent on his side. Implicit in his statements are two criteria which will guide Socrates in his own interrogation of Euthyphro: (1) universality--what is just for one must be just for all, i.e., ethical actions must be universal; (2) disdain for those who do not answer the contradictions latent in their own words.

However, as Socrates begins to guide the discourse, it becomes clear that Euthyphro himself does not reverence these principles in regard to his own utterances, nor does he yet understand that even such claims as can be advanced by a would-be friend of the gods are answerable before philosophic questioning.

At an earlier time in the Greek world this insistence on giving reasons appears to signal a kind of inquisitiveness expressive of a lack of intimacy, bad breeding, or disrespect for the privacy of personal desires. It is not only of Euthyphro that Socrates demands reasons, but in the presence of Euthyphro Plato permits us to glimpse the peculiar way in which Socrates asked questions of himself on the way to taking a stand with respect to those ideas that would make him the most upright of mortals. Socrates asks Euthyphro a question that sets the dialectical process of inquiry in motion: "What is piety?" Innocently Euthyphro responds, "That which I am doing now, prosecuting the unjust man." Clearly this is not at all what Socrates had in mind for an acceptable response. At best it is an example not a definition. Several things have been accomplished by Socrates' question and Euthyphro's response. The question dislodges Euthyphro from his smugness and sense of self-certainty.

We have learned that an example is but an expression of the essence or *eidos* for which Socrates is in search. We might ask a question that is not explicitly raised in the Platonic dialogue: "What is the gain in searching for a definition and what will satisfy Socrates' criteria for an acceptable definition?" The interchange which follows, where the argument joins the question, is instructive in gaining insight into the nature and purpose of questing for a definition.

Euthyphro now responds to Socrates' question with an affirmation that is more global in its reach: "Piety is what is pleasing to the gods." The universality of such a statement as typifying a definition has a benefit, namely that it is applicable at all times and places and binding upon all persons. Therefore, one has gained an insight into the stance to be taken up when one confronts a particular exemplification of the case in question. It was precisely this kind of knowledge that the father of Euthyphro was lacking. And this deficiency, prior to the encounter with Socrates, runs the risk of becoming the intellectual legacy of the son.

Socrates commends Euthyphro on doing better in offering a definition of piety, but indicates that the content of the statement troubles him. For it has only the appearance of universality, and is contested by the known facts. The gods quarrel among each other. What is pleasing to Hera is not necessarily pleasing to Zeus. Therefore, it is necessary to amend the earlier formulation in order to reach a satisfactory definition: "piety is what is pleasing to all the gods." Here, it is tempting to interpret the Platonic Socrates as making a move in the direction of monotheism. This position is buttressed by Socrates' earlier statements to Euthyphro that such myths as impute moral deficiencies to the gods are unacceptable to him. Socrates has in fact told Euthyphro that his unwillingness to accept accounts of the gods acting errantly may well be the reason he has been charged with impiety (6a). The central question concerning the essence of holiness remains to be answered. The knowledge that it is pleasing to the gods does not tell us what piety is, only that is dear to the gods. Only in a formal sense would monotheism represent a response to this question.

At the apex of the dialogue is a riddle posed by Socrates to Euthyphro: "Do the gods love piety because it is pious; or, is it pious because it is loved by them?" This abstract question takes on content when we recognize that if the gods love piety because of intrinsic characteristics about it then there is a limitation upon the gods in so far as they are answerable to that which is holy for gods and mortals alike. Otherwise, if piety is established simply by being pleasing to the gods, then whatever they find pleasing at one time may be subject to alteration with a change of circumstance. In the second case the relation of gods to mortals is that of master to slave. On this view

Prometheus can correctly be said to have been guilty of impiety because impiety was nothing other that the expressed will of the tyrannical Zeus. Can Prometheus have been both just and guilty of impiety? This would not be true if piety is in fact a part of justice and justice like piety has its own essence. If, however, piety does not partake of justice, then it can be argued that the relations between gods and mortals have no bearing on what mortals in common hold to be just.

The question arises as to how one knows whether or not any given set of beliefs, customs, and institutions authentically deserves to be called 'religious.' It is clear that for the Platonic Socrates, since piety is a part of justice, then for a person to be called religious, he must at least be just. Ethical conduct cannot be divorced from religious claims. If Euthyphro is truly a religious man, he must also be a just one. If it can be determined than he is not just, it can also be safely concluded that that he is lacking in piety, and is, therefore, not religious. The reciprocal claim that if one is just, therefore, one is also religious does not follow axiomatically. How shall we know what is just and unjust, what is pious and impious?

In order to elicit the content of piety Socrates advances the question as to whether piety or justice is the more inclusive category. This apparently abstract question has deep practical consequences. The argument is by analogy. It begins with a seemingly innocuous question as to whether fear or reverence is the more inclusive term. Because a Socratic inquiry is always guided and premeditated, though this is concealed by Plato's artistry, it has at times the appearance of ordinary discourse. It is in fact a mimesis or imitation that reflects a peculiar kind of dialectical discussion. Fear is a more pervasive experience than reverence. This point is established when Socrates draws out from Euthyphro the recognition that men fear such things as shame, poverty, and illness. This does not imply that these phenomena are governed by emotions of awe or reverence. Therefore, while every expression of reverence has a core of fear, this is not reciprocally the case. Fear is in this sense more encompassing than reverence. Just in the same way it is established by Socrates that odd is a part of number and not the other way around. What of the relation of justice to piety?

If justice belongs to the domain of ethics or right conduct and piety to religion, then what is in fact being asked is the question: what is the relation of philosophy to religion? If piety is a part of justice, then justice is the careful attention that men pay to other men and piety the careful attention that men give to gods. Thus, at the heart of this inquiry is no less a question than the relation of mortals to gods. Let us review the analogical process of discovery:

$$\frac{Odd}{Number} \div \frac{Reverence}{Fear} \div \frac{Piety}{Justice} \div \frac{Religion}{Philosophy} \div \frac{Gods}{Mortals}$$

It is through reason, especially through the activity of dialectical thought, that such conclusions are to be derived. Philosophy is the constant companion of practical knowledge. Philosophy reigns supreme as the discipline to which all others are answerable. It seems that the gods themselves are respondents before the court of philosophical reason. In so far as mortals become human by exercising their reason, the chaos of the universe is transformed into order and raw strength into a demand for just conduct. Socrates has made an advance over Prometheus, and Plato has adopted a stance far more radical than that of Aeschylus. For it is man whose pursuit of wisdom is divine beyond even the strength that issues from the multiple expressions of divinity in the cosmos. It is no wonder that, according to the standpoint which equates piety with that which is simply pleasing to the gods, Socrates was charged with impiety. For, from this view it seems clear that the charge of atheism against Socrates is a credible one. Yet, as we learn from the *Apology* Socrates insists that he was working in the service of the god, Apollo. Apollo is here simply, however, the personification of reason. The installation of reason as divine makes clear that the philosopher is masking his claim to be a god. If one stops here, it does not make sense--if one takes the words of Socrates earnestly--to engage in the study of anything but philosophy. For it has been established that just in the same way that odd is a part of number, so too is religion a part of philosophy. More emphatically still can the gods be said to have meaning only within the compass of human concerns and understanding. No wonder then that the pursuit of philosophy is more pure than that of religious life. However, and this is not often noted, the dialogue does not end here nor do questions concerning the content of right conduct.

If piety is a part of justice, Socrates asks, what part of justice is it? It is the careful attention that ought to be paid to the gods. What kind of relation holds between gods and mortals? There are two modes of expressing the divine-human relation: asking of the gods and giving to them. The first we call prayer, the second sacrifice. Sacrifice, however, is, upon reflection, as Socrates determines, a paradoxical concept. It presumes that the gods desire sacrifices of which they have need. However, if they are needful, and lacking, then we may conclude that they are imperfect. Hence, they are not gods at all. Implicitly they must desire sacrifices without needing them. This is the first formulation of the paradox that is to become thought provoking to western theology in the guise of the attributes of divine omniscience, omnipotence, and perfection. We can only conclude, as Socrates does, that the argument has moved full circle. The gods express their desires for sacrifice or anything at all only because it is pleasing to them, and not for any other reason. Piety then is that which is pleasing to all the gods. This calls into question the apparent clarity of the analogical argument which concludes with the subordination of gods to mortals and thus appears to return the argument to its beginning. At this point Euthyphro complains that Socrates is talking in circles without benefit and leading him into confusion. This common complaint against all subsequent philosophy is not unknown to the Platonic Socrates.

The *Euthyphro* ends inconclusively. This is true of every Platonic dialogue, and it is properly asked whether this lack of resolution is anything but a testimony to the impotence of philosophy. Yet it should be noted in this instance that it is Euthyphro not Socrates who breaks off the conversation. Moreover, it should be kept in mind that Socrates lets Euthyphro go without having shamed him or having made him cynical of knowing how to act in a just manner. Euthyphro does not appear open to the task of philosophy. Still, Socrates treats him respectfully with a reverent eye to what he might have become if Socrates had left him shattered and without the security of any of his previous convictions. Socrates is divinely moderate in his conduct if not in his expectation.

## II. The Education of Eros: Plato's *Symposium*

The task of the *Symposium* is twofold. The first is to reveal the aspects of eros, love, in its multiple dimensions. The second, as is revealed by Socrates at the heart of the dialogue, is to demonstrate the intimate connection between eros and the task of philosophy. Dialectically, the dialogue unfolds as a series of discourses on love, each speech making arguable progress over the one preceding it, culminating in the speech of Socrates. The positioning of the speakers, the seating arrangements, and the dramatic undertones all evidence the fact that to reflect upon love is at the same time to participate in its work. This is to suggest that the dialogue will reveal more than a simple philosophic description of love. It will show love in action and at work.

Dramatic form plays so central a role in Plato's *Symposium* that the dialectic of the argument on the nature of love appears, at times, almost hidden. Atypically, Socrates must patiently wait his turn until the preceding speakers have held forth on the nature of love. There is no denying that the speech of Socrates is the central one, but it is hard to conclude that Plato has employed the positions taken by the other speakers as merely so many foils. Still, as Kierkegaard remarks, "the final representation of the nature of Eros can hardly be said to inhale what the preceding discussion exhaled."[7]

The dramatic action of the dialogue mirrors an event that is placed in 416 B.C.E., some 16 years before the recounting of the narrative by Apollodorus, friend and admirer of Socrates, who was in turn told of the gathering by Aristodemus. A group of eminent Athenians are assembled at the home of the tragic poet, Agathon, to celebrate Agathon's victory in that year's dramatic competition. Eryximachus, recommends that the participants drink moderately and that members of the assembled company offer speeches of praise in honor of love. Pheadrus, who sits at the head of the table, is asked to give the first speech. It is, as we shall see, an important speech, and one that Plato will not discard in the Socratic summation.

Phaedrus introduces a fundamental distinction between the lover and the beloved. It is eros that motivates human action by stirring in the lover a desire to please the beloved. The mediated recognition, which the lover has of himself, derives from the desire to appear honorable in the eyes of the beloved. Here, Phaedrus introduces an intimation of immortality in his praise of love: "Only such as are in love will consent to die for others." Furthermore, Phaedrus introduces the distinction of honor and shame with regard to love. Love is stimulated, according to Phaedrus, by shame and honor, producing both active and passive modes of apprehension. The passive part is the effect produced in the soul of a lover after having interpreted the impact made upon the beloved. The active part is the action itself performed by the lover. Honor and shame each divide the soul in two.

However, in honor the two parts of the soul are in harmony while in shame the two parts are in discord.

The strengths issuing from the description of eros given by Phaedrus find echo in the *homologia* of the polis. The strength of the city is invoked as supportive evidence:

> What shall I call this power? The shame that we feel for shameful things, and ambition for what is noble; without which it is impossible for city or person to perform any high or noble deeds. (*Symposium* 178d)[8]

The ideal army, Phaedrus subsequently states, would be comprised of lovers. Why? Because death would be prefereable to the soldier-lovers than to see themselves dishonored in front of their beloveds. It is fitting that the speech of Phaedrus concludes with a reflection on the relation of Achilles to Patroclus: which one is the lover, which the beloved? Phaedrus takes exception to Aeschylus portraying Achillles in the role of lover and Patroclus in the role of beloved. It was, according to Phaedrus, because Patroclus chose honor in the eyes of his beloved, thus bringing him untimely death, that the gods chose to accord the most prestigious place to him in the Island of the Blest. This description of love as having "sovereign power to provide all virtue and happiness for men whether living or departed" summarizes the exalted status which Phaedrus ascribes to eros.

Pausanias, the second speaker, agrees with Phaedrus that Love is a great god and benefactor. However, he imposes important questions and qualifications. Pausanias' essential question, which presages a later query of Socrates, is whether love always benefits the beloved. To affirm that love is always beneficial is at the same time to argue that love is always practiced wisely. Just as we might acknowledge that Phaedrus' conception of love harbors certain very contemporary romantic elements, so too, is the division introduced by Pausanias between spiritual and corporeal love a distinction that is widely recognized and appreciated by many in our own day. The distinction advanced by Pausanias is couched in terms of popular and noble love. Noble love is enacted when the lover attempts to benefit the beloved in terms of virtue and wisdom. Popular love aims at immediate gratification of the senses, and is set in motion by attractive qualities of the body. There is, of course, no reason to believe that this popular kind of love will benefit the beloved, nor is there any reason, according to Pausanias, for thinking that it will stabilize.

The spiritual and physical spheres into which Pausanias divides love suggest a certain relational character that belongs to eros. In itself eros, on this account, is neither good nor bad. The relational character of love has a certain relativisitic disposition:

> For of every action it may be observed that as acted by itself it is neither noble nor base. So also it is with loving, and love is not in every case noble or worthy of celebration, but only when he impels us to love in a noble manner. (184a).

In spiritual love, the beloved must be guided by the lover, thereby acquiring an education and a command of all the learned arts (184e). This interval of education is the sine qua non for gratification, i.e., synthesizing the two kinds of love. However, from a purely practical standpoint such equality, symmetry, or steadfastness in the pursuit of love may be lacking. In such a case, foreshadowing the relation of Socrates to Alcibiades, such consummation cannot take place.

There is, however, a more theoretical objection which may be interposed. It is, in effect, the philosophic objection to Pausanias' speech, which Plato permits Eryximachus, the third speaker, to make: "How are the two spheres of love related to one another?" (186b). Eryximachus is cognizant of the necessity to harmonize the two spheres of Heavenly and earthly love introduced by Pausanias. Let us here keep in mind that Aristophanes is the next scheduled speaker. Only an untimely case of the hiccups, to be cured by the medical art of Eryximachus, occasions this disruption of the planned harmony of speeches in praise of love. Eryximachus' solution to the dilemma proposed by Pausanias is the introduction of a third mediating principle, i.e., the principle of harmony. Without harmony the relation between spiritual and earthly love would be purely equivocal. This would mean that what happens in one realm would have utterly nothing to do with what is occurring in the other realm.

Moreover, Eryximachus recognizes that eros does not occur in a vacuum. The relation of the lover to the beloved must not only be a calm, harmonious, and equable one but the relation of the lover to the beloved must stand harmoniously related to the world. Such harmony suggests a quite contemporary holisitic concept of love in which the opposing forces of the universe are themselves compelled by such harmonious principles to act in concert with one another (186b). It is the knowledge of medicine to which Eryximachus has recourse in proving to his own satisfaction the correctness of his essential theory of cosmic harmony as the resolution to the problem posed by eros:

> and the master-physician is he who can distinguish there between the nobler and baser Loves, and can effect such alteration that the one passion is replaced by the other; and he will be deemed a good practitioner who is expert in producing Love where it ought to flourish but exists not, and in removing it from where it should not be. Indeed he must be able to make friends and happy lovers of the keenest components in the body. (186c)

Eryximachus explains that the science of medicine itself is regulated by the principle of harmony.

Drawing on Heraclitus' theory that the cosmos is held together by the dialectic of opposing forces, Eryximachus now applies his theory to athletics, agriculture, and music. The overarching principle of harmony is amplified to include meteorology, astronomy, piety, and friendship. From the concluding statement of Eryximachus, it is evident that Socrates, in his own speech will incorporate certain elements of the praise bestowed on love by Eryximachus. Love for

Eryximachus conceals a cosmology where everything and everyone can be free of strife. It is a world where man can be content, and therefore, at home.

What, then, could possibly be said to be lacking in Eryximachus' description of love? What could terminate such love? The possibility of disharmony threatens the most harmoniously constituted love-relation. It is the ridiculous sneeze of Aristophanes that in curing his hiccups calls in question Eryximachus' theory of erotic gratification and attendant cosmology.

From a strictly dialectical stance, the argument has progressed in the following way: 1) From the speech of Phaedrus it is clear that eros is to be praised for its effects. It is a principle that shows its power, both its benefits and deficits, in the realm of action. 2) Pausanias has made clear that love shorn of its object is ethically neutral, that it is capable of harm as well as benefit. Hence, the separation insisted upon by Pausanias between spiritual and physical love. 3) Both empirical evidence and conceptual demand for unity demonstrate that love is governed by a principle of cosmic harmony. This is the primary dialectical contribution advanced by Eryximachus. In the context of the argument and the drama, the speech of Aristophanes is out of place in a most purposeful fashion.

By rejecting the notion that love is a great god, Aristophanes separates his speech from those of his predecessors. From a narrowly constructed dialectical stance, Aristophanes introduces a new and vital variant characterization of love: "Love is simply the name for the desire and pursuit of the whole" (193a). This dialectical observation of Aristophanes will be preserved in the speech which Socrates puts into the mouth of Diotima. More immediately pressing is the inability of Eryximachus to explain why eros is attracted to one subject rather than another. In point of phenomenological fact, it is often the case that eros flees harmony for sake of a subject, the longing for which is sure to produce disharmony. At the same time, it must be recognized that, in Eryximachus' view, disharmony proves to be the inversion of love. Restlessness and opposition are essential features of dialectical thinking, provoking eros toward objects more worthy of its attention.

Only the search for what is believed to be the completion of one's own self, or what we might call "the Aristophanic other," is sufficient to account for the passion with which eros pursues its object. This observation of Aristophanes remedies a deficiency in the speech of Eryximachus. Within this context, the myth of our ancestors employed by Aristophanes becomes important in framing a distinction between the speech of Aristophanes and the one to be offered by Socrates. From the complexity of Aristophanes' myth it is not clear whether our ancestors were truly "whole" beings. Nor is it clear that the gods could weld us back together even if it were our intention. The myth tells of Zeus' splitting of the original globular humans in half because they attempted to overthrow the gods. Each half appears in a form sufficiently different from the original; it is two footed and erect rather globular. It is, therefore, unclear whether any Aristophanic half could actually have found his other in the time contemporary with Aristophanes' speech.

More critical is the psychological-existential appeal of the myth of the Aristophanic other. Aristophanes asks the would-be lovers (assuming they have found their other halves), if it were technologically viable for them to be welded together by Hephaestus, would they in fact wish for this as their end? Surely, this puts to rest the vague abstractions of Phaedrus and Pausanias with regard to the specificity of the lover and the beloved. Plainly, Aristophanes asks:

> Do you desire to be wholly one; always day and night to be in one another's company? For if this is what you desire, I am ready to melt you into one and let you grow together, so that being two, you shall become one, and while you live a common life as if you were a single man, and after your death in the world below still be one departed soul instead

of two--I ask whether this is what you lovingly desire, and
whether you are satisfied to attain this this? (192e)

Aristophanes' concept of love is drawn from a myth which would
make the attainment of such love an act of impiety. In their original
hybris the globular beings sought to storm Olympus. Their
punishment is to remain forever sundered. The romantic impulse
governing the desire for wholeness contains at least the seeds of a
philosophic argument. The argument, in essence, values the
recognition of human incompleteness and the desire to remedy this
deficiency. The restless quest for the Aristophanic other is dependent
upon the good will of the gods:

> Wherefore let us exhort all men to piety, that we may
> avoid evil, and obtain the good, of which love is to us the
> lord and minister; and let no one oppose him--he is the
> enemy of the gods who oppose him. (193e)

Aristophanes' fatuous myth ends in exhorting piety, of exposing the
hybris of Socrates. For who could be the other half of Socrates? Who
could be the other half of Aristophanes? Two men each in search of
that which is by definition unattainable.

It is imperative that the reader hold in his mind the distinctive
place which Aristophanes occupies in the Platonic imagination.
Aristophanes is more than one more combatant engaging in dialectic
gymnastics. This is the Aristophanes who is cited as producing
evidence of the impiety of Socrates (see *Apology* 18d). Plato was
thoroughly conversant with the plays of Aristophanes, including *The
Clouds* where Socrates is depicted as the proprietor of a think-shop
where the well-born, well-bred young men of ancient Athens learn
how to ridicule their own parents in argument. Socrates wished too
much, according to the play, to be in the company of the immortals, to
usurp their prerogatives knowing full well that his mission was only
ironically enjoined by Apollo. (That is to say, a now shrunken version
of Apollo who represents reason alone.)

# Plato

The comic poet, as portrayed by Plato, stands at a distance from love. Aristophanes recognizes that the distinction between the lover and the beloved is a primal one, the overcoming of which stretches the bounds of piety. Such love is taken up in search of one's Aristophanic other. The comic nature of love is not lost on Socrates. Through his interrogation of the tragic poet, Agathon, the ironic relation of Socrates to eros begins to emerge.

In his exchange with Agathon, Socrates reverts, for the first time in this dialogue, to a dialectical form of enquiry. Agathon criticizes the earlier speakers for concentrating on the effects rather than the essence of love. Dramatically, Agathon returns the discourse to the speech of Phaedrus. Agathon agrees with Phaedrus that Love is a great god. Against Phaedrus, Agathon holds that eros is the youngest of the divinities. Love is not only transcendingly beautiful, but morally excellent, and the consummate expression of temperance, and valor. A typical argument from Agathon would show the necessity of Eros being coincident with temperance:

> Add to his (Love's) righteousness his entire temperance. I may take it, I suppose for granted that temperance is defined as the power to control our pleasures and our lusts, and that none of these is more powerful than Love. If, therefore they are weaker, they will be overcome by Love, and he will be their master, so that Love, controlling, as I said, our lusts and pleasures, may be regarded as temperance itself. (196c)

Socrates lets this sophism pass, readying himself for a more ambitious argument. For in the earlier statement identifying love with temperance, there is merely a substitution of names that proves only that one wished to identify love and temperance at the outset.

Socrates professes ironic admiration for Agathon's panegyric on love. Through a series of rigorous questions, Socrates both enlightens Agathon and sets up his own commentary on love. Socrates has not forgotten the essential question: what is Love?

SOCRATES: I want you to look at Love from the same point of view. Is he the love of something, or of nothing?
AGATHON: Of something, naturally.
SOCRATES: And now bearing in mind what love is the love of, tell me this. Does he long for what he is in love with or not?
AGATHON: Of course he longs for it. (200a)

This constitutes a pivotal move in the argument of the *Symposium*. Love is relational or intentional in character. It is not a substance. It is predicated upon a lack and recognized longing to compensate for that which is lacking. The idea that Love is a god, old or young, is refuted. From the *Euthyphro* we have already learned that gods lack nothing, and from this point of view we should have to acknowledge that "lacking" and "longing," indispensible qualities to love, are foreign to the perfection of divinity (see *Euthyphro* 13b). This does not argue that love cannot be a benefit bestowed by divinity.

Socrates, however, refines the argument: One could desire to possess something and be fearful of its being taken away. In such a case it would be more accurate to say that: "I wish these things now present to be present in the future" (200d). However, the question remains as to the true object of love. Agathon and all of the preceding speakers have in one form or another indicated that beauty is the true companion of love. More Socratically put, it is beauty that love lacks and longs to possess eternally. Agathon is about to be undone by Socrates.

SOCRATES: Ah, your words were beautiful enough, Agathon; but pray give me one or two more: you hold, do you not, that good things are beautiful?
AGATHON: I do.
SOCRATES: Then if love lacks beautiful things, and good things are beautiful, he must lack good things too.
AGATHON: I see no means Socrates, of contradicting you, he replied; let it be as you say.

# Plato

SOCRATES: No, it is truth, my lovable Agathon, whom you
cannot contradict: Socrates you easily may. (201c)

There is a third point conceded by Agathon to Socrates in the
preceding encounter, i.e., that what is truly beautiful is necessarily
good. In sum, then, this vital exchange has established that love is the
desire for the perpetual possession of the good. The good is perforce
the beautiful. And it must be sought, and when achieved, maintained.
The groundwork for the speech of Socrates has now been prepared. It
will become evident that while Socrates inhales less than was exhaled
by the previous speakers, by no means can we conclude that the earlier
speeches were incidental to the dialogue as a whole. A more thorough
study than space allows us would demonstrate that the order of
speeches and the arrangement of the speakers is hardly less arranged
by chance. Still, the consummate portrait of Socrates awaits us both in
the figure sketched by Alcibiades and in the speech of Diotima.

Love has a paradoxical character intimately associated with the
birth and death of philosophy. Through the speech of Diotima, which
is related to the drinking party by Socrates, love is disclosed as having
a dual parentage. Poenia or poverty is the mother of love, a lack that
must be remedied or completed. Love's father, Poros or plenty, is that
after which love strives. The birth of love depends, then, upon the
restlessness which sets it in motion. The consummation of love is,
however, in a certain sense its death. A being for whom nothing is
missing no longer loves. Because philosophy is the love of wisdom, a
completely wise man cannot,then, in a strict sense, be a philosopher.

Love is of the beautiful, and the beautiful is good. Eros is that
which is on its way to being both beautiful and good. Eros is the rift in
nature that makes it possible for nature to be transformed to a higher
plane. Eros is, thus, metaphysically amphibious, bestirring our
inertial selves, and then wakening them to a longing which begets
longing. Here, there is implied an implicit response to and criticism of

Aristophanes. The object of love is *eudaimonia*, i.e., perfection , or alternatively translated as happiness:

> though by my account [says Diotima] love is neither for half nor for whole,unless, of course my dear sir, this happens to be something good. (206a)

The idea that men are unreservedly drawn to the good, in the guise of the beautiful, elicits a key turn in the argument. This is the establishing of the link between eros, beauty, goodness, and immortality. If the good is desired,it must be so perpetually. This affirmation brings a question in its train: "How is eros to achieve the good in the guise of the beautiful in perpetuity?" Diotima's discourse outlines the three essential objects to which eros attaches and therefore defines itself. Each represents a quest for the meaning of life to outlive the length of life, i.e., immortality. Unlike the immortality of the gods who do not change, human immortality must make concessions to human nature. To beget progeny upon the beautiful is what all eros aims at. Where it differs is precisely in what it wishes most to perpetuate.

Biological immortality is common to all living species, at least within the realm of aspiration. Even Socrates married and had two sons. *Thumos*, or the spirited aspects of the psyche, wishes to have its deeds outlast its days. It aims at winning a name that will endure when the person is not. It is the will to forgo many pleasures for the anticipated joy being remembered. Beyond physical children and the rewards of ambition exist the beautiful intellectual progeny of educators, poets, lawgivers, and above all else philosophers. Here, we should be forced to conclude that the literary progeny of Homer are greater still than the accomplishments of the Homer's parents in bringing him into the world.

What has been called the ladder of love speech, which Plato puts in the mouth of Diotima, is one of the most enduring metaphors for philosophy that we have, and here we begin to grasp the full importance of the *Symposium* as a fundmental work both in Plato's career and in the history of thought. The attendant vision of reaching the consummate, perfected illumination of beauty itself to all beautiful beings can be glimpsed as a condensation of Platonic project of philosophy. Diotima's speech not only sketches the ideal way of moving from lower to higher levels of reality,and thererby distinguishing reality from appearance, but also describes the flight of the philosophic imagination. Eros becomes aroused in the presence of one beautiful being. This is surely the first love in which all the world is reflected. To turn from love of one beautiful being to recognizing what is commonly beautiful in many beings (and here Plato seems to mean individual persons) is easier to effect in the realm of speech or *logos* than in the realm of *ergon* or deed. The movement is not merely additive, from one beautiful body to a second and a third, but from one to the indefinite. In concluding that each beautiful body is the same in respect to the form of beauty which gives it its lovely appearance, the individuality of attachment is left behind. This makes for excellent philosophic progress, but difficult romantic attachments.

Each step of the ladder of love speech contains an implicit argument, one that is worthy of examining in its own right. Diotima's summary will suffice us:

> Starting from individual beauties, the quest for the universal beauty must find him ever mounting the heavenly ladder, stepping from rung to rung, that is,from one to two,and from two to every lovely body, from bodily beauty to the beauty of institutions, from institutions to learning, and from learning in general to the special love that pertains to nothing but the beautiful itself until at last he comes to know what beauty is. And if, my dear Socrates, Diotima went on, man's life is ever worth the living, it is when he has attained this vision of the very soul of beauty. (211c,d)

Viewed from a Homeric perspective, the ladder of love speech sublimates eros, *agon*, and *arete*. First, eros is attracted by one beautiful,concrete corporeal being. As it matures, it recognizes that this one being merely partakes in the concept of beauty which informs all beings of their beauty. From a Homeric perspective eros is governed by the goddess Aphrodite. It is to this sphere of eros that the romantic speech by Pheadrus in the opening of the Symposium belongs. Here, the speech of Pausanias, which distinguishes noble from base love, is later incorporated by Socrates. There is a pattern or logic to eros, which the speech of Eryximachus, despite its deficiencies helps to clarify. Eros is open to the possibility of transformation through education. Through experience and education eros can find a more suitable companion to satisfy the longing of its ardor. The desire for beauty in the corporeal domain is not left altogether behind. This is the essential contribution which the speech of Aristophanes makes to the final vision of love presented by Diotima. However, to be called love in a true sense, eros must long for that which is in essence good as well as beautiful. Agathon understands this point, but cannot, when pressed, explain the source of his inspiration. Moreover, he is fundamentally mistaken in thinking that love is a god. Love ends, then, by refuting all of the previous praises bestowed on it by at least five of the previous six speakers (excepting Aristophanes), and transforming its recognized essence.

What then can be said of the essence of love? The object of love is the good which leads to happiness (*eudaimonia*). Happiness consists in the immortal or perpetual possession of the good. That beauty which is the cause of all individual beauty can be glimpsed in the beautiful speech of Socrates. Love is valued and recognized by the object of its longing. In its innocence, beauty inspires a desire for children on the corporeal level. It moves from the sphere of the private, the volatile, and the hidden, into the light of the day of the marketplace. Hera, rather than Aphrodite exercises supervision. Beauty now appears through the refracted light of honor and recognition. The political life with its honors and triumphs provides a more satisfactory monument to the now transformed desire of eros to live in perpetuity. However, as Aristotle will subsequently note, political acclaim is deficient just to the extent that it permits revisionism, the esteem bestowed by others can be transformed into scorn.

It is Socrates who does the proper work of love. The work of love is to show itself. Showing involves seeing and being seen. The work of love is shown by the Socratic interrogation of love, which can be seen, although not necessarily or always directly. Socratic dialectic preserves the agonisitic impulse of the Homeric Greeks while transforming its mode of expression. The wrestling match between men gave way to the collision of opposing forces in the realm of speech. It is through Plato's magnificent artistry that the dialectical undercurrent of the *Symposium* shows itself in the action of the drama.

Alcibiades in his drunkenness sees more clearly the persona of Socrates than do the other revellers in their sobriety. It is not only in discourse that Socrates practices the irony that defines his social intercourse with others. Socratic irony permits Socrates to absolve himself from his own utterances. This is not to say that he disclaims personal responsibility for his statements; rather, the contrary is true. He uproots his interlocutor by the very premeditated ambiguity of a discourse that is never finished, always on its way, pulled restlessly by an unattainable pursuit of perfection. It is through his relentless use of irony that Socrates forces Euthyphro to compare Socrates to his ancestor Daedelus. Socrates makes statements move, just as the statues of Daedelus were so life-like that they appeared to move. Above all, the philosophic ironist says one thing while intending another, not so much to victimize his interlocutor, as to create in his auditors, the capacity for self-reference. To call to the attention of the student an awareness of existential contradiction is by itself a negative moment in the Socratic dialectic. What such philosophic irony opens up is the recognition of existential consistency, a self-attachment that is a precondition for philosophy. To understand justice is to act in a manner that is just. Virtue can be known. The test of its being known is a life that is virtuous. What , then, of love? It means to love that which is worthy of being loved. Socrates, whose very ugliness was awe-inspiring to the ancient Greeks, who praised the appearance of beauty, is portrayed by Plato as eros incarnate, midway between gods and mortals.

According to Alcibiades, the very appearance of Socrates was itself the incarnation of irony. Socrates intentionally drew his students toward him with his awe-inspiring erotic intensity. His intention in doing so was not to make his students dependent upon him. Rather, this is exactly what distinguished Socrates from the Sophists. The Sophists appealed to the *eide* to make their students dependent upon them; Socrates drew his students toward himself in order to push them away toward the *eide*. This is the lesson that Alcibiades recounts as having learned the hard way. He wished to gain wisdom quickly and cheaply by merging with Socrates for a night. But this is not the way in which Socratic wisdom is won. It is through time, by establishing one's own relation with the deathless ideas that one gains an intimation of immortality.

The ironic Socrates is in fact ironic by necessity, which is to say, that only insofar as others appreciate his irony does it have meaning. The philosophic ironist is permitted to write comic poetry which only others can enjoy. From his own side, his intercourse with others is confined to the mode of tragedy. Only with the immortals is he permitted to have non-ironic discourse. This leaves him in a state of perpetual wakefulness and majestically alone. Socrates outlasts Aristophanes and Agathon in discourse and in drinking, even outlasting the dawn. And then he spent the rest of the day in his ordinary fashion; and so, when that next day was done, "he went home for the evening and reposed."

# Plato

## NOTES

[1]See Aristotle's comments on the achievements of Socrates in his *Metaphysiscs*, 1078b.

[2]While we indicated most Greek words with italics, "eros" and "psyche" are common enough to present them as a standard words in English.

[3]Plato is cited, according to convention, by work and division number referring to the printed Greek edition of 1578. These divisions are called Stephanus numbers, referring to the Latin version of the name of the editor/printer of that first edition, Henri Estienne. Stephanus numbers are included in most standard translations.

[4]John Wild, "Plato's Theory of Τεχνη: A Phenomenological Interpretation," *Journal of Philosophy and Phenomenological Research* (March, 1941), pp 255-293.

[5]The translation of the *Euthyphro* used here is by Lane Cooper from *The Collected Dialogues of Plato*, ed. Edith Hamilton and Huntington Cairns, Bollingen Series LXXI (Princeton, N. J.: Princeton Univ. Press, 1969).

[6]Jacob Klein, *Greek Mathematical Thought and the Origin of Algebra* (Cambridge, Mass.: MIT Press, 1968), p. 8.

[7]Søren Kierkegaard, *The Concept of Irony*, tr. Lee Capel (New York: Harper and Row, 1965), p. 78.

[8]*Symposium*, tr. W.R.M. Lamb, in *Plato III: Lysis, Symposium, Gorgias*, Loeb Classical Library (Cambridge, Mass.: Harvard Univ. Press, 1967). In this section parenthetical use of reference numbers are to the *Symposium* in this edition unless otherwise noted.

# Suggested Readings on Plato

PLATO'S WORKS:

*The Collected Dialogues of Plato, including the Letters*, ed. Edith Hamilton and Huntington Cairns, Bollingen Series LXXI (Princeton, N.J.: Princeton Univ. Press, 1969).

> This is the most readily available edition of all of Plato's works with translations by many different hands. There is a general introduction by Huntington Cairns and an excellent index. Brief introductions preface each dialogue.

*The Republic*, tr. with extensive commentary by Allan Bloom (New York: Basic Books, 1970).

> Bloom provides a readable, literal translation of *The Republic* and appends a Straussian commentary. Particularly good on problems of translation and the necessity of maintaining Plato's word-concepts in an English version. Also, a good index.

COMMENTARIES:

Paul Friedlaender, *Plato*, 3 vols, Bollingen Series LIX (Princeton, N.J.: Princeton Univ. Press, 1960, 1969, 1973).

> A pioneering three-volume introduction to the study of Plato. Particular emphasis is placed upon the literary form of a Platonic dialogue, providing important clues for understanding apparently obscure dramatic devices. In addition, the Friedlaender volumes survey the Platonic corpus, drawing the reader's attention to the links between key Platonic concepts as well as showing the thematic and historical relations of the dialogues to each other.

Jacob Klein, *A Commentary on Plato's Meno* (Chapel Hill: Univ. of North Carolina Press, 1965).

> A model of Platonic scholarship focusing on the *Meno*. Klein's commentary is introduced by a general introduction on the interwoven patterns comprising the main structures of a

# Plato

Platonic dialogue. This work provides the contemporary reader with the dramatic and conceptual keys needed to unlock the inner dimensions of a Platonic dialogue. Klein's work also provides a valuable excursus on Plato's theory of *anamnesis* (recollections). The excursus heals to place the *Meno* within the context of the Platonic corpus.

Robert J. Anderson, "The Dramatic Unity of Plato's *Theatetus*," an unpublished doctoral dissertation (Yale, 1976) (currently in preparation for book form publication).

An original reconstruction of Plato's *Theatetus*. The most sensitive integration in English of the dramatic and conceptual aspects of this dialogue, which deals with Plato's theories of knowledge.

Søren Kierkegaard, *The Concept of Irony*, tr. Lee M. Capel (New York: Harper and Row, 1965).

The doctoral dissertation of the founder of existential philosophy. An unusual look at Socratic irony by the modern master of philosophic irony. Kiekegaard is interested in what it meant to think as Socrates thought, to live as Socrates lived, free from our contemporary preoccupation with narrowly drawn and technically addressed philosophic issues.

Jacob Klein, *Greek Mathematical Thought and the Origin of Algebra* , tr. Eva Brann, (Cambridge, Mass.: MIT Press, 1968).

A brilliant reconsideration of the phenomenon of Greek mathematics and its role in shaping the character of ancient as well as modern philosophy. Klein persuasively argues that Plato's conception of mathematical thinking is at the very heart of his theory of reality and how reality can be known. A difficult but valuable work.

Leo Strauss, *The City and Man* (Chicago: Univ. of Chicago Press, 1978).

An intensive examination of Plato's *Republic*. Strauss provides invaluable clues to illuminating obscure passages in the *Republic*. At the same time he provides a profound contemporary reflection on Plato's theory of politics and its relation to his views on philosophy and education. A particularly powerful analysis of the crucial Book I of the *Republic*.

Leo Strauss and Joseph Cropsey, *History of Political Philosophy* (Chicago: Rand McNally, 1963. See especially Strauss's essay, Plato, pp. 7-64.

Strauss makes a most compelling case that Plato's is the first and, he aruges, most important political philosopher. The argument centers on a discussion of the *Republic* and *The Laws*.

Leo Strauss, *Natural Right and History* (Chicago: Univ. of Chicago Press, 1953).

Strauss depicts the fundamental struggle of philosophy as one between the 'ancients' and 'moderns.' Plato is the seminal figure among the ancients. Strauss offers a general exposition of the Platonic doctrine of justice and natural right. Furthermore, Strauss argues that all subsequent ethical and political philosophy is to be measured against the Platonic theory of reality. See the first four chapters in particular.

John Wild, *Plato's Modern Enemies and the Theory of Natural Law* (Chicago: Univ. of Chicago Press, 1968).

Wild presents a compelling argument (directed particularly at Karl Popper's *The Open Society and Its Enemies*) that Plato is not a totalitarian thinker. Coming in the midst of the cold war era, in the wake of the new positivism, Wild's work re-invigorated inquiry into Plato's works as an enduring and invaluable political, philosophic treasure.

Chapter Five

# PURPOSE AND HAPPINESS IN ARISTOTLE:
# AN INTRODUCTION

by Robert J. Anderson

There is no ancient thinker who can speak more directly to the concerns and anxieties of contemporary life than can Aristotle. Nor is it clear that any modern thinker offers as much for persons living in this time of uncertainty. Purpose and happiness are his two dominant themes. The former centers on the concept of final causality--the universe is seen to have a nature such that human beings, and all living beings, are found in a context where life takes on a profound meaning. The latter comprises the theme of the *Ethics*, a book so dedicated to the pursuit of fulfillment and enjoyment that even virtue is understood, not only as the foundation of morality, but as that which is also most pleasant in life. Perhaps it is not too bold to claim of Aristotle's *Ethics* that there exists no other book more directly focused on the achievement of human happiness. And perhaps nowhere else can such wisdom be gleaned so that this goal is made accessible to anyone who chooses to strive towards it.

Aristotle's *Ethics* has its foundation in his *Physics*. There is a natural order for discussing these matters. First the concept of nature (*physis*) should be explicated. This necessitates a discussion as to whether the universe is ruled by purpose or by chance. Out of all of this emerges an understanding of just what final causality is. Furthermore, the locus of final causality in the human domain is the soul. The ancient concept of the soul (*psyche*), in one sense the clearest of notions, has become obscured through history by the sedimenting of Christian and post-Christian layers of meaning. It is the removing of those layers and the rediscovery of that concept that lead to a grasp of Aristotle's unique notions of virtue and happiness.

"Of things that exist", Aristotle claims, "some exist by nature, some from other causes" (*Physics*, Bk II, ch. 1).[1] What does he mean by nature? What are the other kinds of cause? The answer to the first question reveals an understanding of physics that is in utter contrast to that which has shaped the modern world. A response to the second not only helps to clarify the concept of nature but, perhaps more important, it points to the irrevocable limits of human reason and shows the entrance to that realm of darkness that can be illuminated only by faith.

Natural beings, according to Aristotle, are those entities which have *within themselves* a principle of motion or rest. Nature, then, "is a source or cause of being moved and of being at rest in that to which it belongs primarily, in virtue of itself..." (*Physics*, Bk II, ch. 1). Most fundamentally, the natural beings are the living beings: plants, animals, and humans. Secondarily, there are the simple bodies (the earthy, liquid, and gaseous elements, along with fire), which in some analogous sense are thought to move themselves towards their proper places. This principle of self-movement is taken by Aristotle to be the irreducible foundation of all existence and the most proper starting point for all science.

The radical contrast between ancient and modern physics thus becomes clear. Moreover, since Aristotle's views held sway until the very end of the Middle Ages, it can even be argued that Western history has produced two and only two seminal approaches to science. One of them looks at nature and sees growth as being the most primordial phenomenon. The other concerns itself with an analysis of matter and the type of motion that pertains to it. Ancient science obviously lacks the power that results from the technological development of the material realm. But the modern outlook has its own characteristic lack: a frenzied world of unlimited technical progress lurches aimlessly through an abyss devoid of any redeeming purpose.

Aristotle suggests such a contrast in his discussion of the thought experiment of Antiphon. Plant a bed, and what will come up, should the rotting wood manage to send up a shoot? Clearly it will be wood, not another bed. It is the wood, then, that is the real nature; the product of the craftsman is merely an incidental arrangement. Furthermore, the wood itself has the same relation to something more basic. Whatever is most basic of all, the elements of everything else, is at the foundation of this account. It is the immediate material substratum of things that comprises their nature.

But Aristotle turns this account on its head. Of course a bed won't give rise to a bed, yet man is born from man. The former is a work of art (*techne*); only the latter is a product of nature. Art may imitate nature, but it lacks the powers of growth and reproduction. It is these intrinsic sources of movement that constitute the full being of nature. Matter is a necessary concomitant, but it is the form, the organic structure of a living thing, that is the proper subject of physics. This form is the ruling principle of substance. And substance as conceived by Aristotle, in contrast to the modern description of it as material stuff, is the essential being of a living entity. Another name for the form that constitutes a substance is the soul.

If nature is one cause of the things that exist, art is a second. A third is chance. It is in his discussion of chance that Aristotle argues most compellingly for his view that purpose is inseparable from nature. His complex argument can be seen to have three stages. Its conclusion will be that the ultimate kind of causality in the world is final causality, that which is exerted by the natural end (*telos*) towards which things strive.

The discussion of chance begins with the question of whether it is even something real. For a chance event can always be seen to have some kind of cause. Yet there are those who claim that the universe itself came about by chance. "They say that the vortex arose spontaneously, i.e. the motion that separated and arranged in its present order all that exists" (*Physics*, Bk II, ch. 4). If the notion of a vortex is replaced by that of exploding gasses, a substitution that preserves the heart of the claim, the result is a theory that is hardly unfamiliar to anyone nowadays. How does Aristotle attempt to combat this approach?

The first of his three responses is an impressionistic one. He voices surprise.

> For they are asserting that chance is not responsible for the existence or generation of animals and plants, nature or mind or something of the kind being the cause of them (for it is not any chance thing that comes from a given seed but an olive from one kind and a man from another); and yet at the same time they assert that the heavenly sphere and the divinest of visible things arose spontaneously, having no such cause as is assigned to animals and plants. (*Physics*, Bk II, ch. 4)

Aristotle finds such a claim to be absurd. After all, nothing comes to be spontaneously in the heavens, while many things happen by chance beneath them.

This argument, although it has a certain plausibility, is in no way conclusive. The order that is present in the heavens might itself have originated by chance. Thus a second attack will be needed. This one will proceed by means of an analysis of the concept. Aristotle points out that chance is a privative notion--its meaning hinges on the negation of something else. A chance event is one that might have occurred for a purpose but did not. Instead it happened merely incidentally. Even to call it a chance event, however, is to imply purpose, only then to negate it. "It is clear then that chance is an incidental cause in the sphere of those actions for the sake of something which involves purpose. Intelligent reflection, then, and chance are in the same sphere, for purpose implies intelligent reflection" (*Physics*, Bk II, ch. 5).

Now the stage is set for the presentation of an argument that has some cogency.

> Spontaneity and chance are causes of effects which, though they might result from intelligence or nature, have in fact been caused by something *incidentally*. Now since nothing which is incidental is prior to what is *per se*, it is clear that no incidental cause can be prior to a cause *per se*. Spontaneity and chance, therefore, are posterior to intelligence and nature. Hence, however true it may be that the heavens are due to spontaneity, it will still be true that intelligence and nature will be prior causes of this All and many things in it besides. (*Physics*, Bk II, ch. 6)

In other words it is with regard to what is incidental within the cause that an event is said to be by chance. But that which is the cause *per se* will have acted with purpose. Thus nothing can happen by chance without implying some more primary sense in which it involves nature and intelligence.

This powerful argument is still not conclusive. It has shown that the concept of chance is logically subordinate to that of purpose. But what if purposive activity itself has erupted merely by accident? If this were true, then the claim that the universe is characterized by randomness would have to be reinstated. Aristotle, however, in order to develop this most devastating objection to his own physics, is forced to reach beyond the imagination of his ancient contemporaries. It in no way detracts from the meticulous research of Darwin that the great theory which bears his name was actually spun off by Aristotle, several thousand years earlier, as a potential rival to his own view that had to be dealt with. Listen to this brilliant exposition of a thesis which is so thoroughly modern. Remember that the references to "drawing up" and "cooling" express what we would call evaporation and condensation and that the "man-faced ox-progeny" is an ancient description of what is now called a mutation.

> A difficulty presents itself: why should not nature work, not for the sake of something, nor because it is better so, but just as the sky rains, not in order to make the corn grow, but of necessity? What is drawn up must cool and what has been cooled must become water and descend, the result of this being that the corn grows. Similarly if a man's crop is spoiled on the threshing-floor, the rain did not fall for the sake of this--in order that the crop might be spoiled--but that result just followed. Why then should it not be the same with the parts in nature, e.g. that our teeth should come up of necessity--the front teeth sharp, fitted for tearing, the molars broad and useful for grinding down the food--since they did not arise for this end, but it was merely a coincident result; and so with all other parts in which we suppose that there is purpose? Whenever then all the parts came about just what they would have been if they had come to be for an end, such things survived, being organized spontaneously in a fitting way; whereas those which grew otherwise perished and continue to perish, as Empedocles says his 'man-faced ox-progeny' did.
>
> (*Physics*, Bk II, ch. 8)

This is clearly a theory of evolution and it hinges on the notion of the survival of the fittest. Its thrust, however, is the claim that purpose itself is subordinate to chance. Aristotle's response to this objection comprises the third stage of his overall argument. It is in two parts. The first by itself is not satisfactory, except as another formulation of the problem. The second, unfortunately, is expressed somewhat obscurely. This, perhaps, is because the argument it embodies is as difficult as any that philosophy has to offer.

The first part goes like this. All things are either coincidental or purposive. Chance is ascribed not to what happens always or for the most part, but to what happens infrequently. Teeth and all other natural things come about in a given way always or for the most part.

They cannot, therefore, be by chance. Purpose is present in the things that occur by nature.

This argument, of course, will not do. It begs the question. What is really being claimed in the objection is that that which happens always or for the most part is itself the result of chance. Aristotle responds a second time. He states that where a series has a completion, all the preceding steps are for the sake of that. Moreover, as in intelligent action, so in nature, and as in nature, so it is in each action, if nothing interferes. Since intelligent action is for an end, so is the nature of things. While Aristotle goes on to talk of swallows' nests and spiders' webs, the crux of the argument is not exactly clear.

Perhaps this is something of what he is saying. An argument involves a series of steps. A theory involves a sequence of thoughts. The evolutionary view presumes a series of developments. Purpose, however, is said to be a mere appearance; coincidence has brought everything about. But if there is no purpose, how can there even be the appearance of an end? Why should one series of developments be of any more consequence than any other? Furthermore, how would a theory even know how to distinguish the fitting from the non-fitting? Without purpose, would the concept of the fitting even be possible? Moreover, the very act of argumentation itself consists of a series-- why should any one step be any more final than the others? In short, a Darwinian theory, itself the result of anything but random activity, presumes by the very fact of embodying it the notion of purpose it intends to be explaining away.

This argument may or may not be persuasive. At the very least, it is now possible to explicate Aristotle's concept of final causality. Four causes in all are distinguished. The material cause is that out of which a thing is made. The shape of an entity is the formal cause. The primary source of change is called the efficient cause. The final cause is the end, that for the sake of which. But how is this end or purpose determined? It would be easy to posit a divine being which ordained that which is fitting for each natural entity. Aristotle, in fact, argues for the existence of a god, the Prime Mover. However, one thing must not be lost sight of. Aristotle's god is an *unmoved* mover. In other words god does not change in any way; therefore no divine creation of any sort can have come about. God does not work directly by means of efficient causality, but rather only by being the object of desire. How, then, is final causality to be described?

In natural beings, according to Aristotle, the final cause coincides with the formal cause. What does this mean? It means that the end towards which a living thing strives is its very own form--namely the perfection of itself. Thus the final cause of a natural entity, a tree for instance, is simply to reach its own fulfillment, to flourish as a tree. Its end could be called an internal one in the sense that it does not depend on the will of an external divinity to ordain a godly pattern of activity which would then convey meaning. The meaning of life, for Aristotle, is life itself. This might seem deficient in that it lacks any divine confirmation of the worth of a mortal individual. But it also involves that essentially Greek approach in which the purpose of life is the very celebration of life itself. This will have implications for Aristotle's ethics.

The Prime Mover, as has been said, is not the creator of nature. In fact Aristotle, again characteristically Greek, in an incredible display of moderation, will not even ask the question concerning such a creator, a question which had obviously occurred to him. In this regard it is worth returning to an earlier question, that of what besides nature is responsible for the being of the things that exist. Art was a second cause. Its power is derivative, however, since it is itself an imitation of nature. Then there is chance. But chance, the incidental cause, is posterior to that which is *per se*, namely nature. Again, nature is the reality; chance is merely subordinate. Thus there is no other explanation for the being of things. Nature is simply there. No knowledge is available as to a possible creator. Man, as the highest of the natural beings is alone. Human activity has no meaning beyond its own perfection. It is no wonder that Aristotle puts such stress on the joy of fulfilling one's own potential. Beyond this, so far as the rational mind can discern, there is nothing but a vast emptiness. Man can have no direct knowledge of his own creator. Aristotle's stance in the face of this isolation is heroic. Not having been granted a divine revelation, as have other privileged peoples, he guards vigilantly the boundary dividing the fulfillment of rational activity from an emptiness that perhaps only faith can fill.

The link between Aristotle's physics and ethics is his doctrine of the soul. He defines the soul as the actuality of a natural body having life potentially in it. Whatever else may be involved in this definition, it clearly depends on the notion of final causality. Soul is an animating principle, that which enables the natural being to provide its own motion. Such motion aims towards a natural end, its own fulfillment. What is unique about this concept of the soul is its simplicity. One way to characterize it is as the difference between a living being and a corpse of the same species. One cannot assume that such a soul is immortal or can be separated from its body. Nor is it likely that one could deny its existence. It is simply the principle of life in a living being.

Obviously human beings have such a soul. But so do all plants and animals. Thus, while man may be the most highly developed being to have a soul, there is an unbroken continuity from the lowest to the highest entities within nature. Nonetheless various gradations of soul can be distinguished. The main divisions are between the nutritive, appetitive, and rational levels. Anything possessing higher levels will, virtually without exception, possess all of the lower faculties. Human beings, then, having rational activity as their most distinctive function, also have the appetitive and nutritive faculties. This will be an important consideration in the *Ethics*.

Aristotle begins his ethical inquiries by observing that all human activities are thought to aim at some good. What he means here by 'good' must be immediately clarified. First of all the term is initially devoid of moral connotations. Rather it is referring to what is *good for* one. Furthermore, it goes without saying that people are rarely altogether correct in their belief as to what would be most advantageous. Probably the best way to paraphrase the point is to say that all human activities aim at what appears to be advantageous. As a first premise this view might seem persuasive. It must be mentioned, however, that even masochistic behavior can be characterized as aiming at something beneficial, namely the pleasure that attaches to hurting oneself.

This fundamental principle of behavior is the cornerstone on which the entire *Ethics* rests, even the doctrine of morality. As an ethical axiom it manifests a strange blend of the empirical and the prescriptive. It is empirical in that it probes the most basic of human motivations. Yet it is prescriptive in that it posits ideal modes of conduct. Out of this blend comes the concept of virtue, one that is easy to misunderstand. What is unique about this notion of virtue is that it is not a prohibitive moral imperative. Rather it involves a positive approach to life, one which focuses more on fulfillment than on avoidance of temptation.

Granted that all activity aims at that which is thought to be good, just what is it that is most truly advantageous? Aristotle, supposing that all immediate aims themselves point to some more ultimate end, then tries to determine what the chief good would be. His initial answer, however surprising this might be in a work of ethics, is that it is generally agreed to be happiness (*eudaimonia*), namely, living well and doing well. Again, the emphasis is away from that which is prohibitive. But the general agreement he is citing breaks down once one tries to characterize happiness more specifically. Before presenting his own account, he examines several of the most prominent conceptions of the best life. First, one might say that it is a life centered on pleasure. Aristotle rejects this because it would reduce human activity to the level of bestial gratification. Then there is the life of honor. However honor depends more on its bestower than on the good which is being honored. Finally, a life of money-making is rejected for the obvious reason that wealth is for the sake of something else and is not an intrinsic good. What, then, could happiness be?

It is here that the most distinctive insight of the *Ethics* occurs, one which may also be the most controversial. The notions of happiness and virtue are about to be conjoined, in a manner which gives each a unique meaning. In order to achieve a clearer conception of what happiness might be, Aristotle attempts to ascertain the function or work (*ergon*) of man. For if man has a unique work, the human good would seem to reside in it, just as for a flute player, or for any artisan, doing well would reside in the work. But is there such a function or work? Aristotle responds with a set of rhetorical questions. Do the carpenter and the tanner have a work, while man as man does not? Do the eye, the hand, the foot have a work but not man himself? Surely man as man has a function, and the best life would consist in doing this work excellently. The chief good, then, would be activity of the soul in accordance with excellence or virtue (*arete*). But this conclusion needs clarification, especially since all the rest of the *Ethics* will follow from it.

The assumption that man as man has a function must be viewed in the context of the *Physics*. Two things will then become clear. First, since there is no natural knowledge of a creator, no work can be thought to be bestowed on man by a superior being. Rather it is simply there as a part of human nature. Thus the word 'function' is misleading if it suggests a purpose that is determined by some divine agent. Second, there is the question of determining just what such a work would be. This is where the concept of final causality is important. If man as man has a purpose which follows from his own nature, it must be to fulfill his unique capacities. The function of man, then, would be simply to flourish as a human being.

But what would these capacities be? To answer this it is necessary to determine more precisely what is unique about the human soul. To say that the work of man is life is too general; this is common even to plants. Thus nutrition and growth are not enough. Nor is perception characteristic of human beings alone. What remains as peculiar just to man is rationality. Therefore the work of man is to live rationally, and the chief good would be to do this well or virtuously. This is what Aristotle concludes as to the nature of happiness. It consists of a virtuous life of fulfilling one's rational potentiality. But 'virtue' here must be separated from many of its contemporary connotations. It should be understood as meaning human excellence. Achilles was one of the first paradigms of virtue for the ancient Greeks. Happiness then should be seen to consist in the striving for excellence. It is attained as one comes close to fulfilling his or her own nature. And rationality is the essence of human nature.

However, rationality can be understood in two senses. One of these involves the controlling of the appetites and passions, while the other consists simply of thinking itself. Virtue, accordingly, divides into two kinds. Moral virtue is the mind's ruling of the irrational elements of the soul. Intellectual virtue is best characterized by the contemplative life. The *Ethics* speaks at greater length of the former rather than the latter, although it regards intellectual virtue as being a superior mode of activity.

Several points about moral virtue are worth considering here. First there is the role of habit as the essence of moral virtue and an apparent paradox concerning the acquisition of the virtues. Next there is the notion of the mean and what it implies about the nature of happiness. Then there is the discussion of pride, which perhaps more than anything else reveals what is most unique about Aristotle's *Ethics*. Before turning to these issues, however, it is necessary to confront the question of how any notion of virtue can be said to comprise the basis of happiness.

Is it not a denial of common sense to say that virtue is what is constitutive of the happy life? The former seems to imply obligations and strictures, while the latter is clearly something that is chosen voluntarily. It is true that Aristotle distinguishes happiness from pleasure. Yet he also claims that the life of virtue is truly pleasant. How can a set of moral guidelines lead to pleasure? An answer to this question will indicate how different Aristotle's conception of virtue is from most modern understandings ofthat term.

In asking whether man as man has a work, Aristotle made an analogy with the eye, the ear, and the hand, all of which have their own works. Each of these is an instrument. There is a sense in which man as man can also be viewed as an instrument. Happiness consists of being engaged in that specific work for which the human instrument is best suited. Thus excellence and happiness go hand in hand. And virtue for Aristotle is just another name for excellence. Again there is the Greek sense of the joy that is implicit in life--the celebration. Happiness consists of celebrating one's capacities by using them to the hilt. Surely there is pleasure in the graceful functioning of a body and soul which have the potential to perform many wonderful activities. This is the manner in which virtue brings happiness.

But the moral virtues, being states of character, must consist of habitual behavior (the very name of the book comes from the word 'habit,' *ethike*). This leads to a seeming paradox. The way to attain moral virtue is to perform virtuous acts. Yet how can one perform virtuous acts without already being virtuous? A solution can be found by looking at the arts. Just as one learns an art by performing it, through apprenticeship, one becomes virtuous by practicing virtuous acts until they become a fixed part of one's character. In the arts, however, the products have their goodness in themselves. A virtuous act must not merely be of a certain type; its excellence derives from the fact that it is deliberately chosen and that this choice proceeds from a firm and unchangeable character.

Again this simply involves man's fulfilling of his own natural capacities. This can be seen more clearly by considering Aristotle's famous notion of the mean. In everything that is continuous there is an excess, a deficiency, and a mean. But in human passions and actions, just as in the cases of health and strength, both the excess and the deficiency are forms of failure. It is the mean that consititues virtue. What is needed, of course, is not necessarily the arithmetic intermediate; rather it must be approrpriate to the given individual. Such behavior in accord with the mean must become habitual. Virtue simply consists in the performing of these acts--regularly enough to develop skill, and skillfully enough to find enjoyment in them. Thus the mind finds itself at one with its own balanced action. There is purpose and meaning implicit. This is internal purpose. The soul takes such joy in its own harmonious working that it needs no external validation--especially since it is not clear where this would come from.

Aristotle offers a plethora of rich and brilliant insights concerning the traditional moral virtues such as courage, moderation, and justice. Nonetheless, one of the most surprising but also most revealing aspects of the *Ethics* is his view of pride. Not only does he consider it a virtue, thus disagreeing with most modern thinking about morality, but he even goes so far as to consider it a sort of crown of all virtues. It has this status because pride (proper pride) is manifested only by one who thinks himself worthy of great things while indeed being worthy of them. Being worthy he must be good; thus all of the other virtues must also belong to him. Pride, then, (again Aristotle means proper pride) is a sign of the presence of true excellence. But how can a human being, fragile and short-lived, be proud of his own ephemeral existence? It is because there is no knowledge of a creator who bestows meaning on his life; that life itself is the most meaningful thing he knows.

# Aristotle

Yet there *is* an element of the divine in man. This is found in the other form of virtue, intellectual virtue, especially in its highest type which is philosophic contemplation. This is the most noble of activities, not only because reason is the best thing in us, but also because the objects of reason are the best of knowable objects. And if happiness has pleasure mingled with it, Aristotle claims that this is the pleasantest of virtuous activities. However, he goes on:

> But such a life would be too high for man; for it is not in so far as he is man that he will live so, but in so far as something divine is present in him; and by so much as this is superior to our composite nature is its activity superior to that which is the exercise of the other kinds of virtue. If reason is divine, then in comparison with man, the life according to it is divine in comparison with human life. But we must not follow those who advise us, being men, to think of human things, and, being mortal, of mortal things, but must, so far as we can, make ourselves immortal, and strain every nerve to live in accordance with the best thing in us; for even if it be small in bulk, much more does it in power and worth surpass everything. This would seem, too, to be each man himself, since it is the authoritative and better part of him. It would be strange, then, if he were to choose not the life of his self but that of something else. And what we said before will apply now; that which is proper to each thing is by nature best and most pleasant for each thing; for man, therefore, the life according to reason is best and pleasantest, since reason more than anything else *is* man. This life therefore is also the happiest.

> (*Ethics*, Bk X, ch. 7)

With this stirring testimony to the joys of philosophy, Aristotle's *Ethics* reaches its pinnacle. The reader of that work can provide verification of his own, having participated to some degree in the very activity which provides its culmination. And this activity, contemplation, is the actualization of man's highest potentiality, that of thinking. Thus, the person engaged in philosophy (and to a lesser degree when involved with other virtues) attains the end which is also the formal cause of man. He is thereby in accord with nature itself. In this sense man finds himself at home in a world with which he is in harmony. For Aristotle it is enough to work within this realm. Modern science may indeed have rendered man the master and possessor of nature. Since Aristotle's physics is content simply to contemplate that same nature, its aims are perhaps too modest. But the alienated consciousness of Camus' Sisyphus, that proletarian view of work which seems so representative of the modern technological world, would appear foolish to the philosopher who sees work as the flowering of a purposive nature and who thinks happiness to be concomitant with virtuous activity.

# Aristotle

## NOTE

[1]All quotations from Aristotle are taken from the standard translation prepared under the editorship of W. D. Ross. Further citations from Aristotle's works in this chapter are made by work, book, and chapter numbers from this translation.

# Suggested Readings in Aristotle

Much of what Aristotle has written is accessible to the beginning reader. A good general introduction would be provided by all or parts of *The Nichomachean Ethics* and the *De Anima*, along with Book 2 of the *Physics* and Book Lambda of the *Metaphysics*.

However, if time should be more restricted, the following is one recommended list of eleven reading assignments that could be studied in some detail in approximately four weeks:

1. *Physics*, Book 2, chapters 1-3
2. " " chapters 4-6
3. " " chapters 7-9
4. *De Anima*, Book 2, chapters 1-4
   " Book 3, chapters 4, 5
5. *Ethics*, Book 1, chapters 1-5
6. " Book 1, chapters 7-9
7. " Book 1, chapters 10-13
8. " Book 2, chapters 1-5
9. " Book 2, chapters 6, 7
   " Book 3, chapters 1-4
10. " Book 3, chapter 5
    " Book 4, chapter 3
    " Book 7, chapter 9
11. " Book 8, chapters 1-4
    " Book 9, chapter. 9
    " Book 9, chapters 6-8

Chapter Six

## THE BIBLICAL WORLD OF PROMISE

### I. The Created World of the Bible

The Bible has no prologue, no introduction, no preface, (not even an Author's acknowledgement). Where else to begin but with the beginning of creation: *"Beresheis bara Elo(k)im* . . . .In the beginning God created the Heaven and the earth. . . . And God called (to) the light 'Day' and (to) the darkness, He called 'Night.'"

Transforming light into day and darkness into night is, from the standpoint of astronomy and physics, truly miraculous. The narrative account of the first act of creation concludes with the words: "There was evening, and there was morning, one day." What, then, was created in the beginning? A single day that includes night.

The creation proceeds from nothing at all. In the language of medieval theology this is called *creatio ex nihilo* . In Hebrew, creation of something out of nothing is called *Yesh M'ain*. The beginning prefigures everything that follows. Unlike the Greek world that is ruled by *physis* or nature--a world in which the concept of creation is absent, thus making gods and mortals subject to the inexorable order of nature--Biblical creation aims at a purposeful end. The world was created to make a *makom* (place) for godliness to manifest itself. It is man who is positioned in the center of the created world as keeper and redeemer of all the earth.

The Hebraic Bible understands nature itself as creation, created by a Creator who endows the world with logic and gives human beings the capacity to understand the work of creation. God transcends the world which He creates. Therefore the 'natural' world is deprived of its power to rule inexorably over all beings. Creation exists for an end greater than its beginning. It is purposefully rendered incomplete. The work of man is to perfect the world together with his creator. This introduces the central Biblical category of covenant. The covenant is a solemn promise between God and man that includes every living being: "This is the sign that I am providing for the covenant between you, me, and every living creature that is with you, for ever lasting generations: "I have placed My rainbow in the clouds, and it shall be a sign of the covenant between Me and the earth" (Gen. 9:13). To be created means to be promising. The promise of each being differs in relation to its genera and species, as do the multiple colors of the rainbow. Yet, all are held together as one in an arc that stretches between Heaven and earth. Human beings differ precisely in the two-fold character of the promise that is set before them.

The promise that applies to every living being binds the three phases of time together so that the future can be more perfect than the present while preserving the past, even the unrealized possibilities of the past, within it. The work of each being is to realize the divine promise which defines its essence. The promise of an acorn is to become an oak tree. A fruit-bearing tree makes good on its promise by bearing fruit, thereby acting as a fruit bearing tree should.

Man is likened a tree of the field. He also is capable of making his own promises, and therefore, by binding his deeds to his speech, able to create his own future. This two-fold promise both makes man continuous with the rest of creation and places him over the other created beings. The gift of speaking-thinking brings with it the capacity for understanding.[1] The Hebrew Bible is the text through which God reveals the knowledge of his creation to the creature that He makes receptive to such understanding. In the non-tragic world of the Bible, man is given ahead of time all the knowledge necessary to act in a way that will perfect the promise of creation.

In a world-historical sense this present of knowledge occurs in a single hour with the giving of Torah at Sinai (see Bible Appendix ). It is here that the people of Israel are created as a nation, in the event of the giving of Torah. It is this 'hour' of instruction that engenders what in the language of theology is called the 'election' of Israel. To aim at the redemption or completion of creation requires understanding. In the Biblical scheme of history creation exists for the sake of its perfection and completion. This is what is meant by redemption. The giving of the Torah is the phenomenon of revelation positioned midway between creation and redemption. A concept of history where history aims at an end beyond itself is called, in the language of theology, eschatology, from the Greek *eschaton* or end.

The event of the giving of Divine understanding, in Hebrew *Mattan_Torah*, delineates the divine promise through law. Beginning with the Ten commandments and expanding by Rabbinic reckoning to 613 commandments (in Hebrew, *Mitzvot*), the articulation of the contours of the knowledge everyday existence begins. Nearing the land of promise, Moses restates for a new generation the centrality of the giving and keeping of the Torah:

> See! I have taught you rules and laws as God my Lord has commanded me, so (that you) will be able to keep them in the land to which you are coming and which you will be occupying. Safeguard and keep (these rules), since this is your wisdom and understanding in the eyes of the nations. They will bear all these rules and say, "This great nation is certainly a wise and understanding people." (Deut. 4:5-6)

It is this wisdom and understanding achieved through the fulfilling of the laws of everyday existence that the knowledge of happiness and holiness is made possible.

So, unlike the tragic condition of man depicted by the Greeks, man in the Biblical world may suffer still from loneliness, but he is not alone. The very essence of his existence is placed in the sphere that God opens for human understanding. Such an existence requires neither heroism nor philosophy but establishes a democracy of existence, while making room for different levels of understanding. In considering the exodus from Egypt we are reminded that revolution in the Bible exists for the sake redemption through the medium of a teaching, i.e., revealing of the way of man by God:

> Has any nation ever heard God speaking out of a fire, as you have, and still survived? Has God ever done miracles bringing one nation out of another nation, with such tremendous miracles, signs, wonders, war, a mighty hand and an outstretched arm, as God did for you in Eygpt before your very eyes? (Deut. 4:33-34)

The Western roots for our understanding of freedom, justice, and democracy find their essential expression in the outgoing from Eygpt. Tragedy is forestalled through understanding that averts hubris by recognizing the way in which the meaning of existence outlasts its temporal expanse. For even the life of Moses assumes the shape of a promise. He sees the land of promise from a distant hill.

The immediacy of goodness experienced in the primal paradise is compromised in the genesis of man so that the promise of history can be opened for the rest of us. The dream-like atmosphere of innocence is overturned with the first acquisition of self-consciousness. The shame of wakefulness brings the possibility of knowledge, the sweat of toil, the prospect of meaningful work, and with the exile from perfect intimacy with goodness, the pregnancy of historical promise. The crucial turn in Biblical consciousness from the innocence of paradise to the historical awareness of the creation of the nation of Israel takes place in Abraham. Before Abraham it is as if nature still shrouded human understanding in the Biblical world; but in Abraham the implications of the creation for religious and ethical life become human and embodied.

## II. Abraham and the Genesis of Promise

A serious reflection on the Bible can begin almost anywhere. It cannot, however, pass over a reading of chapters 12 through 25 of the

Book of Genesis, which are devoted to the life of Abraham. There are important historical consquences, which alone make this clear. The three great normative Western religions, beginnning with Judaism and including Christiantiy and Islam, all claim Abraham as their father. To reconstruct the attachment of these traditions to the Biblical Abraham is a worthy task. However, it is not the work of our reflections.

Rather, in keeping with our essential thesis that the roots of the Western intellectual and cultural tradition derive from Biblical as well as Greek sources, we shall position our reflection on Abraham within the context of the muted dialogue where conversation breaks upon a long forgotten silence. Who is Abraham? This simple question forms the question of our inquiry. He is a mystery as much as a man. He is a figure embedded in a text, which would make his Author his creator. At the same time he is autonomous enough to make him, in the words of a contemprorary psychoanalyst, "the first modern man."[2]

For Abraham's life is one which presents us with another way of being human from that of Odysseus or Oedipus, Socrates or Aristotle. He is neither an epic nor a tragic hero, nor a philospher in search of himself through reason alone, nor one whose understanding will conform to the natural order of things. For what forces Abraham out of himself is that which is absolutely other. He leaves his father's house to find not the same home reflected with a different meaning, as does Odysseus, but rather, a new land, a new name, a new self, and therefore, a reality not wholly contained in the beginning of his sojourn.

What is incomplete in the life of Abraham cannot be learned by him through truth as it would be revealed by self-disclosure but rather, by that which must be enacted by him or brought into being as a new creation. Viewed from the standpoint of his own temporality, the life of Abraham cannot be a subject for thematization before the very actions that bring about new contents in the world. The promisory structure of the covenant entered into by Abraham with his God reflects a promisory reality that remains to be achieved. Each specific trial that confronts him represents either the speaking of a promise, or its completion, the postponing of this achievement or its apparent compromising.

Beginning with the 12th chapter of the Book of Genesis, Abraham is summoned forth from his home and all of the familial relations which have previously given him self-identity. He is told to go forth from his country, his kinsmen, his father's house, to a land that he will be shown. What summons Abraham forth is not yet disclosed or shown to him, neither the full visiblity of his God, the source of this imperative aimed at him, nor even the land in which he will subsequently find himself.

This one who in his age leaves his country and becomes a wandering Aramaean, and with his descendents after him he moves toward a land of promise which is to form the sacred center of creation. In Abraham who leaves his kindred, the families of humanity open onto history. The fatherless one is to become the father of all: "In you shall all the nations of the earth be blessed" (Genesis 12: 3). From Abraham, who leaves his father's house, the language of being at home through becoming a stranger, and then welcoming the stranger is transformed into the holy gesture of hospitality: "and he lifted up his eyes and looked, and lo three men stood over against him; and when he saw them, he ran to meet them at the tent door" (Gen 18:2).

The universal dimension of Abraham's experience is first expressed in his intervention on behalf of the people of Sodom. The other has already appeared before him in the guise of a country that is not yet his, of the son for whom he longs and who is not yet, and for those with whom he has no intimate relation at all. For Abraham, the work of reasoning, sanctifies understanding: "Surely this be far from you; shall not the judge of all the earth deal justly?" (Gen 18). The covenant of the Bible is enacted as responsibility. The ability to respond is given by God. The enactment of reason is asking for justification and the giving of justice. This reason which sanctifies does so by making itself accountable to the other, for the other. God makes it possible for Abraham and therefore for everyman to have knowledge of Him, just so that he can perform the work for which he was created: "For I have known Him, to the end that he may command his children and his household after him, and that they may keep the way of the Lord, to do righteousness and justice; to the end that the Lord may bring upon Abraham that which he hath spoken of him" (Gen 18:19). For Aristotle, the work of man is the exercise of reason; for Abraham, the work of man is the enactment of justice and holiness.

In this dialogue betwen Abraham and his God, Abraham wrests a concession that is to fire the Hebraic imagination from that time to this, namely that justice is to be enacted by the Judge of all the earth. Abraham has recognized the possibility of injustice, i.e., that it is theoretically possible that: "the righteous shall be swept away with the wicked, so that they shall be as the wicked" (Gen 18:24). To dwell in the absence of justice signifies that justice exerts a claim from without, comes, as it were, from the future. The result of Abraham's conversation with his God is that it will be known to man from this time on that power must be put in the service of justice. God allows himself, indeed asks of man, that He should be made accountable. The mathematics of infinity can be glimpsed in Abraham's attempt to drawn near to the absent others, and to count, along with God, the reality of that which ultimately counts.

In the moment when Abrham draws near to speak with his God a decision to welcome him is reciprocally demanded. The other's relation to me is enacted as moral by virtue of his calling into question of my spontaneity, of my abstract freedom, and thereby, of his asking of me to invest my freedom as a way of responding, or as we would say, of commitment. The promisory character of Biblical language necessitates that action act as the guarantor of speech. In this realm of dual presence and absence, the achievement of simlutaneity or finality does not represent the abstract category of negation, but is lived either as the postponement of death or as the recommencement of life.

Surely Abraham had every right to withdraw himself from the inhabitants of Sodom, with whom he had no obligatory relation. It is his sense of the Infinite that bestirs him and draws him near on behalf of those who are not perceptually near to him. He stands ready to speak. From this dialogue between Abraham and God we are able to see the emergence of the ethical character of Biblical discourse. In this discourse every utterance in the presence of the divine Other, and by analogy all others, is subjected to the rightful demand for continuing justification. The Other, in limiting my freedom by the sign that he gives forth, opens the prospect of attending to the manifestation of a language in which the self is accountable for what it says. This signifying of discourse that shows through language alters the tragic sense of finality where apology is only for the benefit of historians or scholars. Biblical drama from the human side is, then, not prescribed in advance of the beings who enact its promise.

It is however the 22nd chapter of the book of Genesis which narrates the binding of Isaac, in Hebrew the *Akedah*, which most explicitly raises the question of the relation of morality to faith, of ethics to religion, and of the essential relation of man to God. Dramatically, the directive given to Abraham by God, his ultimate trial, perfectly parallels the opening words of God to Abraham found in the beginning of his sojourn from home:

> After these events, God tested Abraham. 'Abraham,' He said; and Abraham said, 'Here am I.' And He said: 'Take now thy son, thine only son, whom thou lovest, even Isaac, and get thee into the land of Moriah; and offer him there for a burnt-offering upon one of the mountains which I will tell thee of.'     (Genesis 22)

All that has been said concerning the ethical character of Biblical discourse is called into question by these words. The core of the existential paradox facing Abraham concerns the relation between the ethically imposssble demand that Abraham should sacrifice his son and the religious obligation to follow the command of God without hesitation or resentment. Kierkegaard in his magnificent work *Fear and Trembling* succeeds in uncovering the dynamism of this episode by revealing the temporal dimension of Abraham's existence.[3] For Kierkegaard reminds us that to appreciate the event we must see Abraham's radically contingent condition as he himself must have experienced it. This means that we must encounter Abraham as he encounters his God, without knowing in advance that the religious command would be countermanded, and that Isaac would be given back to him . An ethical discussion of the event of the binding of Isaac must conclude, as Kierkegaard does, that from the perspective of morality either Abraham is a prospective murderer or he is mad. This is why, according to Kierkegaard, Abraham can speak of God's request to no one, not to Sarah,, not to Isaac, not to anyone. For as we have noted, the ethical dimension of Biblical discourse depends upon the capacity of offering a just explanation to the other who would challenge the spontaneous thrust of my self-assertion. Still, Abraham is neither a murderer nor is he mad, but rather he is called upon to become the father of faith that surpasses the understanding it includes.

When addressed by God, Abraham responds characteristically: *Heneini*, "here I am." This connotes not only a sense of spatial presence but also a sense of readiness, of being prepared and of being oriented. The text also notes that Abraham, as was his custom, "Rose up early in the morning." Still, in the text a journey of eight hours is extended to a period of three days. If we conclude that Abraham knew in advance that he was merely being tested, and that Isaac, the son for whom he had waited a life time, would surely be given back to him, the slowness of the journey would make no sense. We would have to conclude that Abraham was not listening in all seriousness of truth. On the other hand, if we believe that Abraham's condition is one of despair and that the words of God are not easily called back, then we are forced to the conclusion that the convenant, including its ethical core, will surely come to nothing. Will the duration of meaning end with the cessation of consciousness? In Genesis 17 Abraham has already been promised that the covenant realized through Isaac will endure for all generations, that is to say, that the meaning of existence will last longer than life itself.

Exactly here, in this paradoxical imperative, Kierkegaard positions Abraham as first a 'knight of infinite resignation' and then a 'knight of perfect faith.' These modes are more than diverse profiles of a static portrait, but rather define the becoming of Abraham where the knowledge that everything will be lost is circumscribed by the affirmation that everything will be given back.

The very first words we hear Isaac speak in Scripture, breaking this terrible silence which leaves ethical life intact, are advanced to his father Abraham on the three day journey to Moriah: "My father, here is the fire and the wood. But where is the lamb for the offering?" Abraham responds with perfect, systematic equivocation: " 'God will see to a lamb for an offering, my son,' replied Abraham" (Gen 22:8). The text reveals a delicate complicity on the part of Isaac, noted by the Rabbinic tradition, a complicity of faith, which appears to have escaped even Kierkegaard. For surely Isaac, who is not a lad of thirteen years but in his full strength at thirty-seven, could have overpowered his father.[4] The *Akedah* is a trial for Isaac as well as Abraham. And here Isaac offers not resistance or mere complicity but rather a mutuality of faith: "The two of them continued *together*" (Genesis 22:9). For Isaac knows that his God is just and at the same time knows the seriousness of his father and his father's God. With every gesture and every movement the invisible bond and the theoretical discourse becomes more menacingly visible: "He then bound his son Isaac and placed him on the altar on top of the wood. Abraham reached out and took the slaugher knife to slay his son." Just as surely as Abraham's consciousness may be divided, the intent of his action is clear and undivided.

The mortality of Isaac is not altogether unlike that of everyman who would affirm that meaning will triumph over impending mortality. Moreover, he proved himself to be the worthy succesor of his father Abraham, not just by his legacy but by his faith. This is why the scripture refers not to the God of Abraham, Isaac, and Jacob but to the God of Abraham, the God of Isaac, and the God of Jacob. For in each generation the covenant must be reenacted by the lonely man of faith. Isaac, like Abraham, is called upon to distinguish between God and God's blessings. And when those blessings are concealed the light of faith is radically revealed. In fact, one Rabbinic commentary maintains that it is harder for Abraham to remove Isaac from the altar than to place him upon it.[5] Perhaps this is the reason why the full text that Kierkegaard draws his title from is not "fear and trembling" but "rejoice in fear and trembling" (Psalm 2).

Martin Buber has maintained in a chastening rejoinder to Kierkegaard's reflection that the condition forced upon Abraham at the time of the *Akedah* is a theological anomaly from the standpoint of scripture. Buber's words are worth noting for the reader who would put himself only in Abraham's position. For faith is almost always the amplification of moral instruction rather than the engendering of a paradoxical relation. Still, the text upon which we have been commenting remains shrouded in the depths of an infinite mystery. It does in fact contain a sanguine conclusion in which faith is proved to be the surplus of ethical life and not its inversion. "Then an angel called to him from heaven and said 'Abraham! Abraham!'" Everything is given back and redoubled, and from an ethical point of view perhaps more importantly the continuity of ethical integrity is continued in the midst of its interruption. This is the narrative of Abraham, the father. Its monotheism is enacted as ethics before it is reflected to thought, and, then, theology. There is one world, inhabited by many persons, each of whom is called upon to become at one with himself, at one with the others, before the One who is divine.

## III. Jacob: Spirituality in the World

Abraham embodies a unified sense of faith that, however painful in the moment, surmounts the difficulties of the most severe test. His promised fatherhood of nations is practically and spiritually focused in being the father of Isaac. In this he represents both the prospect of eternity and the intensity of familial immediacy. For Jacob, the question of faith is not perhaps so dramatically tested as Abraham's but the paradox of faith is perhaps even greater. Jacob is tested both for his familial life, the twenty years of work for Lavan, that gains him material goods as well as familial fulfillment and for faith in his wrestling with the angel.

> And Jacob was left alone; and there wrestled a man with him until the breaking of the day. And when he saw that he prevailed not against him, he touched the hollow of his thigh; and the hollow of Jacob's thigh was strained as he wrestled with him. And he said: 'Let me go for the day breaketh.' And he said: 'I will not let Thee go except thou bless me.' And he said unto him: 'What is thy name?' And he said: 'Jacob.' And he said: 'Thy name shall be called no more Jacob, but Israel; for thou hast striven with God and men and hast prevailed.' (Gen. 23:25-29)

The paradox of the spiritual and the material is indicated by the fact that scripture continues to refer to him as Jacob as well as Israel after he has wrestled with God and men. These two names, Israel and Jacob, represent the spiritual and the physical respectively. The name Yaakov derives from the Hebrew *Ekev* or heel, and the name Israel from the root word *Rosh* or head.[6] From the very bottom of his heel to the top of his head, from the lowest to the highest, he is called upon to experience the extremes of existence and to remain one. The way of Jacob is *through* the world rather than above it. He stretches time toward eternity, the material toward the spiritual, and the spatial toward the temporal.

Scripture says: "And Jacob went on his way" [Hebrew: *V'Yaakov halek el' darko*]. This statement is emblematic of the way of Israel and his children in general.[7] The way of Israel does not decline as Jacob makes his way back into the world of everydayness. This theme is given particular emphasis when read in conjunction with the characterization that Jacob gives of himself, just after his dream, in his encounter with his brother Esau. About himself, Jacob says: "I have been a sojourner with Laban" [Hebrew: *Im Lavan garti*]. For twenty years he has dwelled with Laban in Haran, which the *Zohar* interprets as "the fierce anger of the world." It is the epitome of exile. Concerning his immense toil for Laban, Jacob remarks, "by day the heat consumed me, and the frost by night." In Haran, the fierce anger of the world, the "sleep fled from [his] eyes," and as he remarks his wages were "changed ten times." Moreover, Jacob is stating that in the midst of his hard toil in an alien place he did not change in the steadfastness of his devotion or purpose. His children do not follow the practices of the inhabitants of Haran. While Abraham and Isaac raised their children in the holy land, and not in exile, still it was possible for them to have children like Ishmael and Esau. In Haran Jacob became a wealthy man in material things. Yet he brought up his sons out of exile whole and complete. The statement to Esau, "I have sojourned with Laban" [*Im Lavan garti*], conveys the sense that while Jacob soujourned with Lavan, he did not become like him.[8] Jacob recognized himself as a sojourner with Laban, a statement which reflects his generalized recognition of the condition of man as a wanderer through the world where the paradoxical dualism of the spiritual and the physical, the temporal, and the spatial serve the world of elevating the profane to the sacred.

Where Abraham's faith fuses all of existence together, Jacob encounters the paradox of existence and the tensions between world and faith. Jacob's twelve sons and the story of the rivalry between Joseph and his brothers is, in one way, an expression of Jabob's conflict between himself and the world, between his present wealth and family and the yearning for eternity. For Jacob and for Joseph a material success is juxtaposed with an exquisite sense of the subjective. The success of Joseph in Egypt comes about, in part, through his understanding of the subjective world of dreams. That success, which brings his father and brothers and their people to Egypt, intensifies the problems of existence that are felt and reflected upon by Jacob. Paradoxically, that success prepares for the dialectical leap that will result in the subjugation of the Israelites in Egypt and the calling of Moses that culminates in the Exodus, the giving of the law, and the forging of a nation.

## IV. Work, Bread and Dreams

It is to dreams that Freud turned first in order to awaken self-interpretation. Dreaming is the threshold of the door between conscious and unconscious life. The symbols of dream-life provide the key for unlocking the door to unknown wishes and fears. Dream life calls for interpretation, because it reveals the unknowing side of the hidden motives, i.e., the psychopathology of everyday life.

Psychoanalysis is advanced by Freud as the cure for individuals to recover reason from the irrational, disassociative tyranny of religious, i.e. neurotic, behavior. The disassociation of conscious and unconscious life is the source of all pathological morbidity. Religion is, however, characterized as present at the creation of human neurosis. This accounts for both the fascination and hostility of psychoanalysis with religion.

For Freud, *Oedipus Rex* is more than a magnificent tragedy by Sophocles. The "oedipal complex" so central to explaining human development and conflict is also the ultimate expression of the relation of self-knowledge to tragedy. In not-knowing, in the non-comprehension of his secret dreams, and buried wishes, Oedipus is to become emblematic of every man, fated to learn through suffering his murderous desires. Oedipus answered the riddle of the Sphinx and supplanted his father as ruler of Thebes. It remains, however, the special privilege of psychoanalysis to explain how man is that being who walks on four legs in the morning, two in the afternoon and three in the evening. For Oedipus this truth, gained in a flash of blinding insight, is learned tragically, that is after the fact, when pain purchases self-knowledge.

Dreams were not unknown in the Bible. Nor was interpretation. "Behold, the dreamer cometh." The brothers sought to slay Joseph on account of his dreams. Joseph is a dreamer, before he becomes a diviner of dreams. It is Jacob (Israel, and the father of the tribes of Israel) who interprets Joseph's dreams: "Behold, I have dreamed yet a dream: and behold, the sun and the moon and eleven stars bowed down to me" (Gen. 37:9).

Is Jacob's response lacking in psychoanalytic understanding? "[W]hat (is) this dream that thou hast dreamed? Shall we indeed come, I and thy mother and thy brothers to bow down to thee to the earth?" Rashi, not surprised by Jacob's immediate grasp the dream's symbolism, only asks about the apparent anachronism of the moon (your mother). "And indeed your Mother is already dead! But he (Joseph) did not know that the words referred to Bilhah who brought him up as (if she were) his mother" (Gen. 39:10).[9]

Scripture records the response of Joseph's report of the dream, Jacob's interpretation, the reaction of the brothers, and the reaction of Jacob: "And his brothers envied him; but his father kept the saying in mind." Just prior to this dream Joseph reports a dream that is even more amenable to the kind of psychoanalytic interpretation presented in *Totem and Taboo*: "And Joseph dreamed a dream and he told (it) to his brothers; and they hated him yet the more." The basis of the hatred of the brothers toward Joseph arises, in the first place, from Jacob's favoritism toward the first-born of his most beloved wife not, in the beginning, from fear of his pre-eminence. And then the dream:

> And he said to them: 'Hear, I pray you, this dream which I have dreamed: for, behold, we were binding sheaves in the midst of the field and lo, my sheaf arose, and also stood upright and, behold, your sheaves bowed down to my sheaf.' (Gen. 37:36)

Rashi notes the apparent redundancy in the phrases "My sheaf arose. . . And also stood upright." The first phrase indicated "It [Joseph's sheaf] stood erect." This phallic imagery could be interpreted as indicative of Joseph's desire for potency, and in the second instance as his wish to displace the brothers by strength of his continuing potency.

The response of the brothers indicates that the power to understand the intent of dreams belongs to them as well as to their brother and their father: "And his brothers said to him: 'Shalt thou indeed reign over us or shalt thou indeed reign over us?'" Their reaction, as recorded by scripture is, therefore, understandable: "And they hated him yet the more for his dreams and his words." The reduction of the interpretation to one of mere sexual potency proves premature. It reduces the phenomenon of being morally 'upright' to being physically 'erect.' That the two are more than imagistically related is indicated by their immediate proximity in the text. The attempt to fashion morality out of psychology ends, however, in explaining neither. What does psychological dominion mean to the oppressed? Take the example of food alluded to in Joseph's first dream. Dreaming about food when there is nothing to eat is a poor solution for the hungry. Psychoanalysis works better for the well-fed. Understandably, it is does not offer the appeal to physical hunger that Marxism does. Rashi, following the statement of the sages concludes about the 'moon' in Joseph's second dream: "And there is no dream without absurd words."

# The Bible

Joseph, nonetheless, rises to pre-eminence in Egypt because of his capacity to interpret and act on the prophetic power of dreams. It is because he acts in a manner that is 'upright,' according to Rabbinic interpretation, that he becomes 'erect.' He descends into the servtitude of his dreams (*cholom*). Through his prophetic dream interpretation, he stores bread (*lechem*) for his father, his brothers, and all of Egypt. By his work (*loichem*) he distributes bread to those who are hungry, and, thereby fulfills the prophecy of his first dreams.

In the midst of his first rise to power as master over the house of Potiphar, Joseph appears first in the light of his standing in order to frame the attempted seduction by Potiphar's wife which results in his imprisonment. "And he [Potiphar] left all that he had in Joseph's hand; and having him, he knew aught save the bread which he did eat" (Gen. 39:6). Rashi comments that bread (*lechem*) here refers to his wife, and then hastens to add "but [the text] speaks with a decent expression." The description of Joseph as a "beautiful form" and his subsequent response to the first attempts at seduction ("neither hath he [Potiphar] kept back anything from me but thee, because thou art his wife") clearly evidence Rashi's interpretation.

There is even here Talmudic opinion that Joseph was going "to do his work" implying, to lie with her. "And it came to pass on a certain day, when he went into the house to do his work" (Gen. 39:11). Rashi comments on the words *l'asos malachto* (to do his work):

> [There is a difference of opinion between] Rab and Samuel.
> One said *Malachto* (denotes) his actual work, and the other
> said (*Malachto* denotes) to live with her, but there
> appeared to his the image of his father's appearance etc.,
> we find in tractate *Sotah* (Fol. 37).

Translated into psychoanalytic language, "The image of his father's appearance" equals the assertion of his superego warding off that which is taboo, i.e. in ordinary language, his conscience alerting him to danger. In this case that which is 'taboo' is adulterous union.

147

It is commonly held Rabbinic opinion that while the Patriarchs lived before the time of *Mattan Torah*, the giving of the Torah, that they were aware of and bound by the commandments. This would include adultery and incest, forbidden forms of sexual relationship. Joseph's behavior is, then, when counterposed to that of Reuven, the oldest brother, understood as God-fearing. Joseph had asked Potiphar's wife during her earlier imprecations: "How then can I do this great wickedness and sin against God?" (Gen. 39:9). Other commentators offer cogent, alternative explanations of the verse: "And having him, he knew aught save the bread which he did eat." Areyeh Kaplan who translates the passage more idiomatically: "[His Master] left all his affairs in Joseph's hands, except the food he himself ate." Kaplan comments: "This is because the Egyptians considered food touched by foreigners to be contaminated."[10] When Joseph, just prior to the reconciliation with his brothers sets food before them, he sends the attendant Egyptians out of the room. Kaplan, absorbing Freudian terminolgy, translates: "The Egyptians could not eat with the Hebrews, since this was taboo to the Egyptians" (Gen.43:32). The Hebrew *lechem* (bread) is specified as the food which Joseph set before them."

It was through his work (*loichem*) that Joseph gathered the resources to fill the grainaries during the seven years of famine. Joseph proves himself an able and unexacting administrator. It is this bread (*lechem*) that Joseph is able to set before his brothers.

But, it is in his capacity interpreting dreams and not as dreamer that Joseph is first elevated and distinguished through Pharaoh's dreams; scripture states "There was no one to interpret them for Pharaoh" (Gen. 41:8). The *Tz'enah Ur'enah* comments: "No one could offer him an interpretation that his heart would accept, for he had dreamed the dream, together with its interpretation. The dream he remembered but not the interpretation."[11] This discovery of unlocking the meaning of the symbols of dreams, not merely understanding their centrality, is decisive to the psychoanalytic exploration of dreams. The analyst is concerned with the self-interpretation(s) of his patient. This is crucial to psychological auto-emancipation.

Earlier Joseph had given an intimation of his own understanding of the work and limits of dream-interpretation. When pressed by the Pharaoh's wine-steward and baker: "We each had a dream and there is no one here to interpret it." Joseph responds: "Interpretations are God's business...If you want to, tell me about [your dreams]" (Gen. 40:8). About his interpretation of Pharaoh's dreams, scripture states, "as he interpreted it, so it was" (Gen. 41:13).

For dreams belong in the inner world, the subjective experience, which can be illumined. Still, work involves the transforming material conditions, "It is by the sweat of your brow that you shall eat your bread." The inner and outer worlds, the subjective and objective, are included within the broader horizon of 'reality.' This is true of the Greek world as well as the Biblical world, and this concept of reality joins the ancients together against the moderns. Reality is, however more than the dreams and work it includes. That is to say, our interpretation of the world falls short of reality, and in turn our capacity to transform the world cannot eradicate subjectivity. More precisely, human individuals in "eating bread" consecrate or desecrate reality, day by day.

The understanding of the mode of sojourning and of the dualism of body and spirit, dream and work, is a necessary stage on the way to the greater drama and realizations of the Exodus. The life of Jacob and its successful elaboration in the world by Joseph provide the essential link between the inward certainty of Abraham and the religious and historical transformations guided by the instruction given to Moses. With this turn toward the Exodus Biblical reality moves to a fullness that was latent in the lives of Abraham and Jacob.

# RECLAIMING THE HUMANITIES

## V. Human Freedom and Revolution in the Biblical World

--And proclaim liberty throughout the land unto all the inhabitants thereof. (Lev. 24:10)

[Alternate translation: "You shall sanctify the fiftieth year, declaring emancipation [of slaves] all over the world."]

Our contemporary ideas concerning human freedom derive from Biblical rather than Greek sources. We are not speaking here of such abstract deliberations of free-will versus determinism as are found in Book III of Aristotle's *Ethics*. Rather, we are speaking of the most immediate and concrete expressions of freedom from physical oppression and the most elementary kinds of human liberties, freedom from hunger, from physical torture, from the invasive violation which slaves suffer from their masters.

Yet, it is exactly in the name of human freedom that three of the most influential critics of religion agree in their conclusions, if not in their analyses. To Nietzsche the very idea of God is forced "obedience toward one whom they say deserves submission." Powerlessness, in Nietzsche's analysis, turns necessity into a virtue. The idea of divine power robs human beings of their own capacity to freely will their own divine destinies.

For Freud, the idea of God is advanced, by complicated turns, to make man feel secure in a world and indifferent to his own aspirations and concerns. Religion, in the title of one of his books, is "the future of an illusion." The emancipation from physical bondage in Egypt is soon replaced by the psychologically induced self-oppression that, born out of guilt, projects a benign Father governing a secure and ordered world, answering the limitless demands children place upon their parents.

Marx, perhaps the greatest modern student of material oppresion, would have done well to have studied the dynamics of the first great historical revolution, which we today call by its Greek name the "going out" or the exodus from Egypt. Religious institutions may well be put in the service of a reactionary state, thereby stupefying, coopting, and making ever more servile the toiling masses of exploited workers. The Exodus is the ultimate model or paradigm of every future revolution. It contests Marx's essential thesis concerning religion that religion by definition and historical example is always politically reactionary and oppressive. At the same time the event of the Exodus is a genuinely revolutionary text that incorporates Marx's critique within a more inclusive, existential horizon. We shall now proceed to examine some of the themes that make the Exodus through a careful reading the most contemporary of revolutionary texts.

The Book of Beginnings, Genesis, ends on a note of high promise. Israel has settled in the land of Goshen, a people dwelling prosperously and apart. Joseph, next only to the Pharaoh in Egypt in temporal power, is reunited with his aging father and reconciled with his estranged brother.

The oppression with which the Book of the Exodus opens is, therefore, all the more stunning. Yet it cannot be construed as tragedy in the Aristotlean sense of a sudden and unexpected reversal of fortune or fate. For the future of Israel was told to Abraham, that his descendants would live through the dark night of exile (Gen. 15:11).

In the crucible of exile a people is transformed into a nation. The Book of Exodus in Hebrew is called *Shemos* or names, which is the first major word-concept in the text: "Now these are the names of the sons of Israel, who came into Egypt with Jacob; every man and his household they came." And they increased: "And the children of Israel were fruitful and multiplied and waxed exceedingly mighty and the land was filled with them" (Exodus 1:8). The seventy souls that went down to Egypt with Jacob are now a people becoming a nation.

The apolitical atmosphere of Genesis changes dramatically as force comes to limit the future of this emerging nation: "Therefore they set over them taskmasters in order to afflict them with their burdens" (Exodus 1:11). The very word Egypt derives from the Hebrew root word for limit (*tzar*). It is the midst of the greatest temporal power in the world that the limitless promise of Israel that was first given to Abraham is tested.[12]

What happens in the dream lassitude of paradise must now be recapitulated. Just as shame and honor enter the world only upon the end of innocence and the recognition of nakedness, so too is this now true in the historical-political sphere of an entire people. Knowledge that is oriented toward action springs from self-awareness. Now it is material oppression rather than spiritual innocence that prompts forgetfulness of the self. Moreover, knowledge of one's own self is, here, dependent upon knowledge of others. The task is no less than to create a bond of solidarity in which is focused a collective understanding of class, nation, and society. The confrontation with political power through material subjugation produces political self-awareness.

What is the quickest way to forge a self-conscious people aware of their collective destiny? For physical, economic, and political oppression, intense suffering expresses the material condition of Israel in the exile of Egypt. Moses learns to his chagrin that a systematically oppressed people must come to an awareness of their own class-consciousness. After the daring, revolutionary act in which he risks his princely privilege, and even puts his life in danger to spare his fellow Hebrews, he is greeted not with gratitude but with the fear and anger that accompany an atomized slavish mentality: "And he went out on the second day, and behold, two men of the Hebrews were striving together" (Exodus 2:13). And is this not the way of oppressors, to have their slaves at each other's throats in order to conceal from them the source of their oppression? Solidarity is a precondition for the expectation of social freedom. Yet, it is not solidarity, but atomized seriality (each for each, each against each) that Moses encounters.

152

"And he said: 'Who made thee for a (man) a ruler and a judge over us? Thinkest thou to kill me, as thou didst kill the Egyptians'; and Moses feared." Moses' fears were justified.

It is not Moses, not the Israelites who demand freedom, but God Himself. A slavish nation is not yet fully adult, not yet fully capable of taking responsibility for its own destiny. Freedom, in fact, must be achieved by a people who recognize the source of their collective oppression. Moses, perhaps remembering his bitter experience in his first attempt to bestir the people years earlier, asks God who has summoned him to go back to Egypt, to lead them out: "But they will not believe me. They will not listen to me. They will say, God did not appear to you" (Exodus 3:4). Moses is filled with justified trepidation in the midst of the theophany that occurs by the bush that burns without consuming itself.

In the outgoing from Egypt, the Torah reveals the radical relationship of God to human freedom. The essence of the idea is expressed in the founding 'commandment' of the first "Ten words": "I am the God your Lord who led you out of the land of Egypt, out of the house of bondage." In this commandment, expressed in the declarative mode, the God of Israel identifies Himself in relation to the deliverance from bondage in Egypt, and by implication the paradoxical imposition of human freedom.

The God of freedom binds Himself to the event of the outgoing from Egypt, i.e., to a concrete historical event. The idea of liberation and the phenomenon of history are expressed in the same statement. A distinctive concept of history is being advanced here. History surpasses the chronology it presupposes. Time past, present, and future must be bound together in a unified whole.

God begins his self-revelation by binding Moses to time past through the medium of the covenant: "I am the God of your father, the God of Abraham, the God of Isaac, and the God of Jacob" (Exodus 3:6).[13] The absent past is preserved in the present. Everything is preserved, possibility as well as actuality. The oppression in Egypt is not senseless suffering. Just as it has been anticipated and told to Abraham in the Covenant between the Pieces, so too its redemptive power will now be realized. As Joseph says toward the close of his life: "I am dying. God is sure to grant you special providence and bring you out of this land, to the land that he swore to Abraham, Isaac, and Jacob" (Gen. 50:24). The covenant is itself the bond between Heaven and earth expressed through the unifying action of time.

It is the future that orients and shapes the meaning of the present in the Hebraic world. Moses persists in his questioning, perhaps even tempered by skepticism:

> So I will go the Israelites and say, 'Your fathers' God sent me to you.' They will immediately ask me what His name is. What shall I say to them? (Ex. 3:13).

The response given is one of the epocal Biblical statements, eliciting voluminous philosophical and theological commentary. Rashi translates the statement made by God to Moses in the future tense: "I will Be Who I Will Be" (Ex. 3:14). While there are differences as to whether the statement should be rendered in the present tense ("I am that I am" according to Maimonides and Aquinas), there is virtual unanimity in the commentary tradition over the meaning of the utterance in its immediate context. Rashi says it means "I will be with you" in the *Yetzias Metzraim*, i.e., in the outgoing from Egypt.[14]

Clearly, it is the future that is now bound up with the present, giving renewed direction, guidance and orientation as well as immediate deliverance. The promissory character of the covenant is now given a dimension that defines existence itself. In His self-revelation God explains to Moses: "This is what you must say to the Israelites: 'I-will-be sent me to you.' " What kind of response is this? Is it systematically ambiguous or perfectly equivocal? Does it contain any content or is it merely thought-provoking? While a full examination of these questions surpass the scope of the present reflection, it can be concluded with certainty that here there is clearly a redefinition of the covenant enacted with Abraham, with Isaac, and with Jacob.

There is a two-fold promise expressed in the statement "I Will Be Who I Will Be." The declaration is itself puzzling because of its repetition. Repetition in this most economical of texts is never merely redundant. What kind of promise is, then, being made by God to the Israelites? It is a promise that affirms that the future itself is aiming at goodness. The distance between the incomplete present and the future to be perfected has itself the shape of promise. How is this known? God says: "I will be," that is to say "I promise." I promise (you) that "I (am) Promise."

This two-fold promise binds word and deed, the theoretical and the practical. In chapter six of Exodus, this divine promise of redemption is amplified.

> Therefore say to the Israelites (in My name) 'I am God. I will take you away from your forced labors in Egypt and free you from their slavery. I will liberate you with a demonstration of my power, and with great acts of judgement. I will take you to myself as a nation, and I will be to you as a God. You will know that I am God your Lord, the One who is bringing you out from the Egyptian subjugation. I will bring you to the land regarding which I raised My hand, (swearing) that I would give it to Abraham, Isaac, and Jacob. I will give it to you as an inheritance. I am God.' (Ex. 6:6-8)

Rabbi Bechaye notes that there are four distinguishable dimensions to the promise of redemption. The first promise as R. Bechaye notes concerns freedom from toil at the hands of the Egyptians. [*V' hozasi*-- lit. "I will bring (you) forth."] As R. Bechaye notes, the sages maintain that they stopped laboring six months before the exodus.[15] The cessation of forced labor is the first concrete act of emancipation. The second promise concerns freedom from the political mastery and domination exercised by the Egyptians. [*V' galti*--"I will rescue" (you from their work).] Hence, the positive autonomy is, by implication, promised here for the first time. An historical nation with its own freely-willed destiny is initiated in the realm of speech. Force will join understanding to bring this about. Clearly, this is a revolution initiated *from above* where the shackles of physical slavery and political subjugation must be thrown off from below.

The completion of the revolution from above cannot be complete because "so long as the master is alive the slave trembles that the master will come and enslave him once again."[16] Hence, the relief of the Israelites at the drowning of the Egyptians. The revolution will not be mere reformation or respite. [*V' lakachti*--"I will redeem."] Freedom from economic exploitation, political tyranny, and threat of murderous revenge are necessary preconditions for meaningful work, political autonomy, and psychological stability: "I will bring you forth from the burdens of Egypt" (*V' hozatsi*). Yet, freedom from such limitations is still to be transformed for the sake of higher end. The fourth dimension of the promise has several levels of its own: "I will take you to Myself as a nation, and I will be to you as God" (*V' lakti*). Here is introduced the much-mentioned, little reflected on 'election' of Israel at Sinai. The giving of the Law, the event of *Mattan Torah* is promised. What is affirmed here is that the way of existence inscribed in Torah is itself promising.

For there to be trust and hope, courage and faith, existence must itself be both personalized and promissory. The idea that the future can redeem the imperfections of the past and the incompleteness of the present is the ultimate horizon within which Biblical reality is formed. It is the interior dimension of human existence rendering religious life credible. This does not mean that the future will necessarily be better than the past. Such a mechanistic concept of history reduces the Biblical concept of Promise to the Enlightment notion of 'progress.'

Such a reduction compromises the radical nature of human freedom and thereby robs history of the full depth of its moral dimension.

As R. Bechaye notes, the Torah is *Morashah*, "heritage" or "bequest" rather than *yerushah* (inheritance) regarding the land of Promise. This distinction is itself open to multiple interpretations. R. Bechaye indicates that the generation leaving Eygpt will not live to inherit *Eretz Yisrael*, the land of Israel, but rather the land will be bequeathed to their own children as an inheritance.[17] This interpretation does not, however, account for Rashi's generally accepted opinion that the women (as opposed to the men over the age of twenty, save Joshua and Caleb) who left Eygpt would themselves inherit the land.

From a more existential standpoint, the very incompleteness of the future suggests that the concept of Promise reveals the way in which the Infinite makes itself manifest within the finite. For even Moses, about whom the Torah says, "there arose not a prophet like him from that day to this," glimpses the Land of Promise from a distant hill.

The category of Promise is inescapable. This does not mean that life can be unpromising or compromising, but rather that it cannot be neutralized or narrowed to the point where there are no expectations. True, this would safeguard against dashed hopes and meaningless suffering. But, then we should be unable to distinguish tragedy from comedy, pain from pleasure, justice from injustice and in the last analysis having lived from never having been at all.

Something remarkable is taking place. The outgoing from Eygpt is at one and the same time the radical revolution of human freedom that culminates in the public knowledge which God gives of Himself and his creation just 49 days after the first day of the Exodus.

This is the event of *Mattan Torah*, the giving of the Law, for the sake of which the outgoing from Egypt occurs. In a broader eschatological scheme, as Franz Rosenzweig frames it, creation exists for the sake of Revelation and Revelation exists for the sake of redemption. In the event of *Mattan Torah*, the past and the future become pure presence.

The divine dialectic leading from *Yetzias Metzraim* is a movement from the finite and limited to the infinite. Still, it is to be accomplished through the material of oppression and the birth of revolutionary political emancipation, the class of masters shares the mantle of authority without giving up the power of privilege. Only a people that thirsts for their freedom will drink from the well of redemption. The gods of Eygpt, not unlike the gods of Athens, must be overthrown.

The sufferings of a slave-people intensify when they make demands upon their masters. Dispersion and intimidation are the weapons which any Pharaoh used to break the will of an incipient rebellion:

> That day (the day Moses and Aaron confront the Pharaaoh) Pharaoh gave new orders to the peoples, administrators and foremen. He said: 'Do not give the people straw for bricks as before. Let them go and gather their own straw. Meanwhile you must require them to make the same quota of bricks as before. Do not reduce it. They are lazy, and are protesting that they want to go sacrifice to their God. Make the work heavier for the men, and make sure they do it. Then they will stop paying attention to false ideas.'
> (Exodus 5:6-9)

Let their labors become intensified, let them see that protest ends in surplus suffering, and above all let them understand the futility of their work. Here are intimations of Sisyphus-like labors. You will achieve the same as before, over and over, but with greater effort and more torment. The fault is yours, not ours. And you will be isolated from one another; "The people spread out all over Eygpt to gather stalks for the straw" (Ex. 5:11).

The desired result is achieved. The leaders complain to Moses and Aaron that conditions have worsened and that they, as instigators, are to be blamed: "You have destroyed our reputation with Pharaoh and his advisors. You have placed a sword to kill us in their hands" (Ex. 5:21).[18]

## 1. From Oppression to Freedom

In Hebraic psychology emotions tend to be drawn down to their purest states. Fear and love are inescapable expressions of human withdrawal and attachment. When the Talmud states that everything is in the hands of heaven except the fear of heaven, it links human freedom with the overcoming of false fears and a vigilance directed towards the source of genuine fear. "Fear of God is the beginning of wisdom" is more than pious homily.

The Israelites, in their enslavement, feared Pharaoh's power, more than they feared God. It was through intimidation that fears are reinforced and manipulated. According to Rabbinic tradition, the practice of idolatry was widespread during the Exile in Eygpt. While the Israelites clung tenaciously to their sense of personal and social identity, even in bondage they kept their Hebrew morals, refused to don the apparel of the Egyptians, and abstained from acts of immorality, still they succumbed to worshipping foreign gods.

The concept of idolatry has been explained in the following way by Kierkegaard. It means making something absolute which is not absolute, or in more abstract language, the absolutizing of a particular thing, person, animal, or object. In daimonic love this can occur between two persons, as we learn from Socrates in his rebuff of Alcibiades in the *Symposium*. The beloved becomes a diety, thereby divesting the lover of his freedom to love that which is beyond possesion and being possessed.

Rashi explains that the Pharaoh's power over his people derived from exactly such daimonic self-deification. When God tells Moses to "Go to Pharaoh early in the morning, and you will find him at the Nile River" (Ex. 7:15), Rashi stresses that the reason for this detailed instruction lay in the fact that Pharaoh had deified himself, and claimed that he neither ate nor drank, nor had bodily needs. Every morning he would go to the Nile and take care of his bodily needs when no one could see him.[19] Accosting him at the Nile, Moses confronted Pharaoh de-mystified of his divinity and divested of his controlling public persona.

It is a well known Talmudic dictum that God does not make unnecessary miracles. Unnecessary miracles would compromise the logic of God's own creation. The suspension of the laws of nature depend upon a prior recognition that 'nature' has an inherent logic, given by God. The inversion of the 'miraculous' is the deification of nature and the natural. Moses' confronting the Pharaoh at the River-god, the Nile, has the added benefit of de-mystifying what was so dear not only to the Egyptians, but the Greeks from Homer to Aristotle, de-mystifying the idea that reality is that which is given by Nature for the sake of things to realize their own natures.

The ten plagues play a pivotal role in transforming the fear of Pharaoh into a fear of God, that is the beginning of liberation as well as wisdom. As R. Bechaye points out there is a precise logic to the plagues, a logic governed by the concept measure for measure (*mida kneged mida*). It has elements of both retributive and revolutionary justice: "They forced Israel to draw water for their animals, and so God turned their water to blood and the animals could not drink."[20] Consider just two examples: Compare this retributive justice to the counter terror and liberation that the Midrash ascribes to the logic of the plagues which are analogized to the way in which a warrior lays seige upon a city: "First he attacks the water supply hoping that without water they will be forced to surrender . . . Next, the warrior has his army make a fearful noise in order to make the populace panic, and so too God sent the noisy army of frogs." Just as the Egyptians "forced them to awaken early, leave their beds and go to work, so God sent frogs into their beds and they would not let them sleep."[21]

# The Bible

The most troubling of all the plagues for Rabbinic interpretation is the plague of darkness. There is general agreement that some of the Israelites as well as their Egyptian oppressors perished during this plague. There is disagreement as to numbers. One opinion holds that fewer than one-fifth of the Israelites lived to experience the exodus and the rest perished during the three days of darkness.[22] Rashi comments that it was during the plague of darkness that Israelites who did not wish to leave were killed so that the Egyptians would not see their deaths and say "They are being punished just as we are."[23] When did this darkness occur? At daybreak, just as the night begins to fade. It is then clearly stamped as a darkness caused by God. How can darkness kill? The text says "even darkness that may be felt." Why is this darkness so terrible that it is the penultimate punishment that Pharaoh relents unconditionally ("take your children") until God hardens his heart? Why is Moses so emboldened: "Our cattle shall also go with us; there shall not a hoof be left behind?" Why does Pharaoh use the language that he does: "Get thee from me, take heed to thyself, see my face no more; for in the day thou seest my face thou shalt die?" He will not see Moses face to face again, but it is the Pharaoh who will die. With an irony that surpasses that of Socrates Moses answers: "Thou hast spoken well; I will see thy face no more" (Ex. 10:28-29).

The theme of night is retained in the ultimate punishment: "About midnight will I go out into the midst of Egypt, and all the first born in the land of Egypt shall die." Some clarity is brought from the plain surface of the text: "they [the Egyptians] saw not one another, neither rose any from his place for three days, but all the children of Israel had light in their dwellings" (Ex. 10:23). The Torah specifies in their dwellings (as opposed to "in the land of Goshen") to indicate that wherever an Israelite lived, even in the house of an Egyptian, he had light and the Egyptian was in darkness. The Lubavitcher Rebbe concludes: the Israelites could (at last) see the Egyptians and could, in turn, not be seen by them.

161

# RECLAIMING THE HUMANITIES

The spell of the 'look that steals existence' (as Sartre calls it) had at last been broken. The master keeps the slave under the search light of surveillance day and night. The slave is made timid by the gaze of the master. Now it is the Master who turns away his face: "you shall see my face no more." He recoils in the terror in which he previously ruled and reposed.

The night of Exile is coming to an end. To know 'darkness' means that night is itself the end which does not lend to dawn. It is, therefore, experienced with trepidation. Homer knew this well. When the great heroes among Greeks are sent out as spies in Book X of *The Iliad* , even Odysseus and Diomedes, they are afraid of the dark. There is "rosy-fingered dawn" but no equivalent metaphor of such beauty to describe the dusk. For even 'night' must be called in to being: "and God called to the darkness 'night.'"

It is at sunset that Odysseus weeps when captured and quite enthralled by the charms of Kalypso all the day. It is Plato, after all, who recognizes the singularity of Socrates, the man who can contemplate both tragedy and comedy, for he outlasts all the other speakers in the *Symposium* and, filled with wine, goes about his usual business, after comedy and tragedy have yielded to the night.

But, the Israelites do not merely endure the night. They act, on God's command at dusk, and break through the limitations of the night to a new and radically different kind of day, the night of freedom that expects the day of knowledge.

They are not motionless in time. "This month shall be the beginning of months to you." This is the beginning of Spring which will, forever, correspond to the event of the out-going from Egypt. The first *Mitzvah* or commandment, preceding the last of the plagues, commences with the numbering of time. In servitude time is experienced as the eternally recurring image of the past. An opening onto the future, the capacity to reorient the past in relation to the present is now possible and is, therefore, mandated.

# The Bible

## 2. The Revolutionary Justice of the Exodus

What remains to be reflected upon is an analysis of the economic dimension in the revolution in Egypt. The surplus value of Israelite labor, the difference between the economic value of the work produced by the class of slaves and the surplus that is drawn and taken by the ruling class from its workers. The text supports in detail the fact that the workers are given only what is necessary to sustain them minimally. Moreover, the means of production are retained by the ruling class so that the class of slave-workers are both dependent upon their rulers for minimal subsistence and unable to accumulate any wealth (capital) of their own. In a feudal, agrarian society the means of production are quite primitive, though no less controlling in determining the capacity to produce wealth. "Now they will gather their own straw."

The re-appropriation of surplus value by the Israelites is the revolutionary means by which the wealth produced by their own hands is achieved. It is not only unleavened bread (*matzah*) that the Israelites carry with them on their shoulders on their way out of Egypt. At the time of the plague of the killing of first-born Egyptians, there is not only an implied overturning of the law of primogeniture, the convention by which the first-born males inherit and control wealth--both capital and the means of production. There is also a massive transfer of wealth. The promise made earlier is now redeemed:

> I will give the people status among the Egyptians, and when you all finally leave, every woman shall borrow articles of silver and gold as well as clothing, from her neighbor or from the woman living with her. You shall load this on your sons and daughters, and you will thus drain Egypt of its wealth. (Ex. 3:22)

How did the Israelites know where the Egyptians stored their valuables? "The Israelites, however, had light where they lived" (Ex. 10:23). Rashi claims that it was from this light that the Israelites could

163

see what was hidden, but could not themselves be seen. The slave unmasks the economic power of the Master.

All that remains is for the political authority that keeps a place in this economic infrascructure to be overthrown. The final act of retributive justice is accomplished as an economic revolution. The threshold of self-empowerment has become too dear.

> The Egyptians were also urging the people to hurry and leave the land...The Israelites (also) did as Moses had said. They requested silver and gold articles. God made the Egyptians respect the people, and they granted their request. [The Israelites] thus drained Egypt of its wealth. (Ex. 12:36)

Is this just? If it were not for Joseph, the Egyptians would have succumbed to starvation long ago. Whose wealth is it anyway? It is the surplus value of the labor extracted from the Hebrews during the 210 years of enslavement.

The Master must understand the nature of his injustice toward the slave. Otherwise, the matter could be construed as merely greater force subduing lesser force. The Pharaoh does more than eat his own words. He acknowledges, under seige, and for a brief but revealing moment the justice of the demands of the oppressed:

> Pharaoh sent for Moses and Aaron during the night, 'Get moving' he said. 'Get out from among my people--You and Israelites! Go! Worship God just as you demanded! Take your sleep and cattle, just as you said. Go!' (Ex. 12:31-32).

The revolutionary structure of authority has changed hands. The same Pharaoh who asked Moses with contempt "who is your God?" now in his last words to Moses petitions him: "Bless me too!"

Now, it could be argued from a Marxist standpoint that this was a purely nationalist revolution, affecting only the Israelites. If so, then why does the text tell us that "a great mixture (*erev rav*) (of nationalities) left with them" (Ex. 12:40). This group, according to two Rabbinic commentators, numbered over a million, and was, therefore, even larger than the 600,000 adult Israelite males who left on foot.[24]

Moreover, this is a perpetual revolution here which is non-utopian. There is neither a classless society, nor a dictorship of the 'proletariat,' except perhaps in the unique sense in which the Levites (to be the priestly class) are forbidden to own land, and therefore eat and prosper according to the will of the people. Moreover, this revolution is spared the anthropocentric humanism which Marx draws from the materialistic thrust of the latter stages of the scientific revolution. "When you come to the land that I am giving you, the land must be given a rest period, a sabbath to God" (Lev. 25:1). Not only the land, but animals shall benefit from this revolution. This is detailed in the link established between *Yetzias Metzraim* and the repetition of the commandment concerning the Sabbath:

> Observe the Sabbath to keep it holy, as God your Lord commanded you. You can work during the six weekdays, and do all your tasks, but Saturday is the Sabbath to God your Lord, so do not do anything that constitutes work. (This includes) you, your son, your daughter, your male and female slave, your ox, your donkey, your (other) animals, and the foreigner who is in your gates. Your male and female slaves will then be able to rest just as you do. You must remember that you were slaves in Egypt, when God your Lord brought you out with a strong hand and an outstretched arm. It is for this reason that God your Lord brought you out with a strong hand and an outstretched arm. It is for this reason that God your Lord has commanded you to keep the Sabbath. (Deut. 5:12)

Areyeh Kaplan, commenting, notes:

> The earlier generation had experienced the Sabbath with the (*Manna*) (Exodus 16:26) and therefore merely had to remember it. However, the generation that would enter the promised land, who Moses was addressing, would, henceforth have to 'safeguard' the Sabbath.[25]

The phenomenon of transmitting understanding from one generation to the next is not unique to a revolutionary generation. However, the challenge of retaining the enthusiasm as well as the content of the teachings given by a generation of founders is perpetual. It is, among historians of religion, a commonplace, but no less an enigma, that Judaism is the most enduring, continuous of world religions, by the most conservative estimates 3300 years from the time of the Exodus. (Maoism, which claimed the attention and allegiance of one-quarter of the world's population, appears not to have outlasted its founder.)

From oppressive toil emerges meaningful work. The pressure of daily work is linked inseparably to the rest of the Sabbath day. Hence, in reiterating the commandment concerning the Sabbath the text states: "Remember that you were slaves in Egypt." The first detailed commandment, the laws for which reasons are given (*mishpatim*), after the event of *Mattan Torah*, not surprisingly, concerns itself with the laws of servitude: "These are the laws that you must set before (the Israelites)." "If you buy a Hebrew slave; he shall serve for six years, but in the seventh year, he is to be set free without liability" (Ex. 21:1). Who is this servant? The commentators hold that the verse refers to a boundman who has been sold by the *beis din* (Rabbinic court), because he robbed and did not have the money to repay his theft. Despite this, his Master may not give him difficult or dirty labor, nor force him to work at night.[26]

Beyond this he had rights that are far-ranging and detailed. Moreover, as the *Tz'enah Ur'enah* asks, why begin the code of laws with a law of buying a Hebrew servant? Because it is intimately related to the first commandment: "I am the Lord your God who brought you out of the Land of Egypt." The commentary adds "that is, to serve Me, and not to work as a servant to [My] servants."[27] Why is the slave who chooses to stay with his Master stigmatized? "I am fond of my master, my wife, and my children; I do not want to go free" (Ex. 21:5). It is

166

because he is denying the mandate inscribed in the founding commandment to live as a free man. "I brought you out of servitude," and by, implication, into freedom. Why is this man stigmatized in such a manner: "Standing the slave next to the door or doorpost, his master shall pierce his ear with an awl"? Because, he heard this with his own ear at Sinai. Why should he go out in the seventh year? "Just as we rest on the Sabbath to commemorate the fact that God created the world in six days and rested on the seventh, so shall a boundman serve his master for six years and go free in the seventh."[28]

In the realm of toil, the phrase "to serve Me" encompasses all the days and nights of the year. It may reasonably be asked: is this not the mere substituting of one form of servitude, however subtle, for another? Even consider God as the ultimate Employer:

> God spoke to Moses, telling him to speak to the Israelites and say to them: There are special times that you must celebrate as sacred holidays to God. You may do work the six weekdays but Saturday (literally, "the seventh day") is a Sabbath of Sabbaths. It is a sacred holiday, when you shall do no work, wherever, you may live, it is God's Sabbath. (Lev. 23:1-3)

At a minimum, this means on 52 days and nights of the year there is no work. With all special days in the year taken into account, there are seventy days of material and spiritual rest mandated. Marx would have done well to treat the first revolution with full seriousness.

### 3. Ritual, Action, and Reality

In preparation for the outgoing from Egypt, the Israelites are commanded to ready the *Korban* (sacrifice) of the *Pesach*, the Paschal Lamb. As in so many other ways, the world of the Bible thus presents the means to comprehend a greater reality that is to come. Here, the rituals are established that will permit both understanding for the participants and remembering for the descendants of the the great events and implications of the Exodus. Sacrifice, giving to the gods, is from a psychoanalytic standpoint the propitiating of project anger that stems from introjected guilt.  It is a form of ritualized behaviour in its generic features as common to the Homeric Greeks (see the end of Book I of *The Iliad*) as it is to the Hebrews.  Even the arch-rationalist Socrates is forced to explain such behavior in the Euthyphro.  Socrates there describes sacrifice as a gift to the gods as opposed to prayer which means asking of them.  If the gods are perfect, then they have no need of sacrifices, yet find them pleasing, as a means of receiving honor.

The *Korban Pesach* contains elements, which, when interpreted from a psychoanalytic perspective, call basic psychoanalytic assumptions into radical relief.  Here it is the object of the sacrifice, its content and not simply its structure, that sets it apart and makes it illuminating.  Joseph's brothers had to be sent from the room where he provided bread for them because "the Egyptians could not eat with the Hebrews, since this was taboo to the Egyptians."  In general the Egyptians were cautious about defiling themselves by eating with strangers.  Kaplan points out they were specifically careful with the Hebrews "because the Hebrews ate sheep, and hence their mouths and utensils were considered contaminated, since sheep were sacred to the Egyptians."[29]  Why, then, did God command the Israelites to take "a lamb for each of their father's homes?" (Ex. 12:3).  Just because they worshipped sheep.  But the Egyptians already knew that the Hebrews ate sheep.  This is why the text says: "An unblemished lamb," and one of "one year" thus qualifying it, by Egyptian lights, as a suitable god, an object for idolatry.  Why was the lamb roasted over fire?  R. Bayche comments: "because that gives off a strong smell, and it was done whole on a spit, to ensure that the Egyptians recognize that it was lamb, yet they were powerless."[30]  Why at dusk?  The *Tz'enah Ur'enah* comments: "They must slaughter the sacrifice between day and night, when everyone is returning form work and can see their idol being slaughtered."[31] At dusk, the end of one day (the long day of exile) and the time just before night (the beginning of the day of deliverance).

Why in their father's homes? It is their fathers whom they are to honor and with whom they have to make peace. Rather, against Freud, it is the gods of the Egyptians who are to be incorporated through the act of eating. And this is not done secretly, but in the most public possible manner. The Egyptians shall also know the meaning of the affirmation: "You shall have no other gods before Me."

The remembering of the outgoing from Egypt culminates in the psychological de-mystifying of the gods of Egypt. What began with the first plague as the muddying of the waters of the Nile River-god with blood culminates in the death of every first born in Egypt, even to the house of the Pharaoh. Now, it is the eating of the gods of Egypt that represents the consummate act of humiliation.

Ritualizing of the outgoing from Egypt is pre-meditated as well as elaborately detailed. This self-conscious externalizing of action serves several interrelated ends. In the first place a symbol system contemporary with current conduct binds conscious understanding to the creation of a community. "You may not carry forth any of the flesh away from the house" (Ex. 12:46). As one contemporary commentator notes:

> The moment that the group sat down to partake of the Paschal lamb, no individual member could leave this group and join another. The feast of Passover was to be celebrated in the midst of one's family and close friends to symbolize the close links that bound together the entire 'family' of the Jewish people. Going off by oneself to eat the Paschal Lamb would therefore signify an act of isolation contrary to the spirit of the Passover.[32]

The atomizing of the Israelites through oppression, placing one against the other, had already been transformed into thorough collective suffering into a *groupe enfusion*. This positive celebration represents a higher level of community which binds the freedom of one to the freedom of all.

Moreover, given the objects to which the conscious intentions of the ritual are expressed, the *Korban Pesach*, the bitter herbs, recalling the embittering of the lives in Egypt, the unleavened bread, i.e. 'the bread of affliction,' are all designed to exteriorize, and therefore make more palpable and real, an inner, experienced condition. The movement from thought to speech results in action only when the deed is enacted self-consciously. Whereas in psychoanalytic interpretation, the exteriorizing of knowledge from thought to speech effects catharsis and confessional self-understanding, the world of action is left theoretically suspended. This means that each one decides for himself alone. Self-knowledge on the psychoanalytic model and knowledge of the world external to self are found in two separate domains, just as is true for Sophocles' *Oedipus the King*.

In readying the Israelites for the event of the knowledge of God, given through the Torah, the problem of transmitting such knowledge to future generations is already reckoned with before it becomes a problem. "And you shall tell your son on that day" (Exodus 13:8). This is made very explicit in the Book of Deuteronomy where Moses is reminding the generation that is to go into the land of Promise:

> In the future, your child may ask you, 'What are the rituals, rules, and laws that God our Lord commanded you?' You must tell him, 'we were slaves to Pharaoh in Egypt, but God brought us out of Egypt with a right hand. God directed great and terrible miracles against Pharaoh and all his household before our very eyes. We are the ones He brought out of there, to bring us to the land he promised our fathers, and give it to us.' (Deut. 6:20-23)

The event of the Exodus is used as supreme example of ritual. It is enacted contemporary with the event. This integrates the conscious with the unconscious, thereby integrating ego with superego and id

170

before disassociation can set in. Event, psyche, people, past and future are made one.

## VI. Justice and Holiness

How, then, shall we now explain what religion is? The Biblical God did not, after all, create religion but rather the world. What makes religion different from philosophy? The philosopher has a task that has remained essentially the same from the time of Socrates. It is to justify the world to himself in the presence of other people. This philosophic task confused the men of the ancient Athenian democracy. To the majority philosophy was not distinguishable from sophistry. Sophistry is the art of persuading other people of the truth without necessarily having to explain to oneself what the truth is. Philosophy is rather self-explanation. The self belongs to the world and the world inhabits the self.

It is in the name of philosophic reason, in one guise or another, that the great critics of religion and therefore of Scripture have advanced their respective critiques. The work of Marx and Freud is to rescue reason from theological sophistry. Among the great critics of religion, no one has provided a more powerful and enduring analysis than Nietzsche. We are today still awaiting a response. Let us first distinguish, however briefly, the difference of Nietzsche's critique, what is unique in it, from the analyses of Marx and Freud, for Nietzsche's analysis combines and absorbs elements of the psychoanalytic and Marxist reductions. If it is the least familiar of the three, it is nonetheless the most radical critique known to us of religious aspirations, pretentions, and institutions.

More readers are familiar with the slogan drawn from Nietzsche's diverse writing, "God is dead," than with the theory behind the slogan and the possibile consequences issuing from it. For Nietzsche, our age signifies not only the death of the word-concept 'god,' but more sweepingly the death of all absolutes. It is a time when "the earth has become unchained from its sun" and when the hour of 'eveningland' is at hand. It is a time dominated by the experienced sense of the aimless relativity of all things, moral, cultural, and philosophical, a relativity that invades the religious domain as well. Ours is a time when it is increasingly difficult to find believable the drama of everyday existence. Nietzsche characterized this experienced sense of the aimless relativity in all spheres of existence as nihilism (nihilism from the Latin *nihil*, nothing), a time when no thing appears to have dominance over any other thing.

Our everyday language is at a loss to explain what our theoretical grasp of the world has evidenced centuries earlier: "Our earth has become unchained from its sun." Does the sun rise and set? From the standpoint of astronomy the answer is a clear and unequivocal no. This conclusion, however, leaves us utterly, if subliminally, going nowhere. It represents the necessary neutering of human experience. The orient is becoming dis-oriented.

We are, upon reflection, forced into an unacceptable choice: to believe the world of our senses, thereby falsifying what experience has learned from theory, or to blindfold ourselves by believing our theories and thus discrediting our sense of experience. The very act of thinking becomes a matter of faith. In the age of the scientific world view seeing is not believing. Believing is not seeing. Do you see the sun rise and believe at the same time that it is rising? Then either you know nothing of scientific modernity or you choose to believe while closing your eyes to the knowledge that your seeing-believing is without foundation.

The more closely you look, the harder it is to find the semblance of what is usually called "reality." This overwhelming sense of arbitrariness is the first registering of self-consciousness in the contemporary world. Fashion is the only father of necessity. A colorless, odorless, impenetrably neutered world stands with frozen indifference against the background of timeless, empty space.

# The Bible

Nietzsche sees dreadful consequences in the contemporary world that would blind even the Greek seer. Reality: what is it? We see a fatiguing moral melodrama; it is rather, for Nietzsche, only a game of craps that Zeus shoots with himself--a game that we understandably choose, governed by the desire to live, to call morality. This greatest modern student of the ancient Greek world, Nietzsche, has one overriding goal: to reestablish the divinity of man, to make of man a great god. Within the context of a neutered world, even the most superficially grand achievements of technological man are reduced to neutered inconsequence. Nietzsche strives to reclaim man and his world.

With great subtlety Nietzsche argues that the history of philosophy represents a veiled and insidious rationalization, a theodicy, which cloaks itself in the seemingly neutral categories of grammar and mathematical coordinates. The cloaked structure of this rationalized existence is an unconfrontable, and therefore undeniable, reign of power over meaning. Marx's whole critique of the traditions of society and religion is an extended meditation on the effects of the ascendency in modernity of power over meaning. While psychoanalysis is content with unmasking rationalization, which masquerades as reason, Nietzsche sees all reasoning as rationalizing, cloaking its failure of nerve in the transparency of declarative discourse. Every reason advanced for every argument presented masks a tacit reference to the Reason of all reasons. Justice, the cornerstone of Western morality, is forged out of the passion for revenge against those forces that incontestably determine our destinies. Time and again Nietzsche warns us against the preachers of justice and equality:

> The desire for revenge has been the subject of man's best reflection to date. . . . To overcome the desire for revenge, that is the bridge to the highest hope, and a rainbow after long storms.[33]

And of love Nietzsche says, that it is not the solution but the problem: "The world is becoming a madhouse, all in the name of love."

The overwhelming experience of arbitrariness is contested by Scripture in the intimacy of imperative discourse, the evidence of a certitude between the holy one and the people Israel who are called upon to become a "holy people." Scripture provides us with an experience of grammar that seeks to rectify, not falsify, the grammar of experience. Let us briefly explore the Biblical grammar which establishes the relationship of power and meaning.

The world here is made visible through the three basic kinds of adjectival pronouns: mine, ours, Yours. The realm of the 'mine,' i.e. my spontaneity and therefore my power, becomes elevated to that of the 'ours' through the study of philosophy. Here in the ours is morality. Justice belongs to everyone. It is shared, public, and knowable by all. It is the realm of reason, argument, and community. Grammatically, it is expressed through declarative discourse. The ours may be as personal as friendship or as impersonal as science. The conception of the ours depends upon an underlying unity, harmony, and homogeneity of the world.

In the realm of the ours reasons are given for conduct, and where reasons cannot be found or advanced, we are no longer in the world which we might wish to call 'ours.' In fact, when we slip out of the ours, we either diminish or stretch the universe. In our universe the 'my' must remain attentive to the ours, so that I might take my turn, or rather so as not to miss my turn. (Our word 'universe' derives from the Latin words meaning 'one turn.') And all such turnings revolve within a shared world. From a Biblical standpoint the ten words on the tablet and those immediately foliowing, the *mishpatim*--the commandments for which reasons are given--belong to the realm of the ours. The central theme of such laws is justice or *tzedek*.

> And if one man's ox hurt another's, so that it dieth; then
> they shall sell the live ox and divide the price of it; and the
> dead also they shall divide.    (Ex. 21: 35).

The realm of the ours is continuous in time and space.  The text upon
which we are commenting shows how the ours binds men to each other
and does not stop even at the threshold of death.  The *mishpatim*
include the several attributes of justice recongnized by Aristotle, the
distributive, the commutative, and the retributive.

> And a stranger shalt thou not wrong, neither shalt thou
> oppress them, for you were strangers in Egypt.    (Ex.
> 22:20).

Here, as in the other *mishpatim*, a reason is given: "for you were
strangers in Egypt."

The Biblical language of the sacred commences with the capacity
to elevate the realm of the ours to that of the Yours.  For the words
mine, Yours, and ours are not interchangeable.  The surplus of the
Yours that includes the ours is the language Biblically expressed as
holiness.

Situated in the geographical center of scripture are the laws
pertaining to holiness, *kedoshim*.  So central is the understanding of
holiness that R. Hiyah taught:

> This section was spoken in the presence of the whole
> assembly because most of the essential principle of Torah
> are attached to it.   R. Levi said:   Because the ten
> commandments are included in them.[34]

If we compare the *kedoshim*--Leviticus, ca. chapters 19-23--with the
*mishpatim*--Exodus, ca. chapters 19-23--we cannot help but be struck
by the virtual repetition of content noticed by R. Levi.  The *mishpatim*,
the laws for which reasons are given or are easily adduced, are
inseparable from a teaching in which freedom is installed as justice.
These laws are recognizable in their contemporaneity.  It is reasonable
to assume, as does Saadya Gaon, the great nineth century Rabbinic
philosopher, that in an infinite time reason unaided would come to

such conclusion of its own volition. The gift of instruction at Sinai is a concession to human finitude that forestalls the inevitability of tragedy by providing in advance a teaching adequate to the exigencies of human life. This is the essential structure of knowledge which frames self-understanding in the non-tragic world of the Bible.

The *kedoshim*, however, in addition to restating the essential expressions of the *mishpatim* , introduce laws for which no apparent reason is given or adequate to their expression. In Hebrew such laws without reasons are called *chukkim*. The very absence of reasons, for Rabbinic understanding, is both essential to their unintelligible essence and vital to comprehending the phenomenon of holiness. There is yet a third category of biblical laws, *eidem* (derived from the Hebrew word for 'witness'), which bear primarily on ritual behaviour and serve the purpose of mediating between the purpose of recalling and reenacting the *mishpatim* and the *chukkim*.

The several categories of laws are not always neatly distinguished. At times, they appear bound together in such a way that each interpenetrates the other two. In part, the *kedoshim* serve to remind us that at a certain level, all of the commandments (*mitzvoth*) are *chukkim* in the sense that there is a limit to our ability to rationalize their meaning. For here justice is enacted as holiness, just as holiness must also be expressed as justice.

In our attempt to rationalize this text as a teaching, by calling near those critics who demand distance for the sake of freedom, we are ourselves not free from responding to the charge of Nietzsche that in religion only a grammar of power is being chiseled into meaning in order to impress the powerless into service. Shall we still say that the sun rises and sets, and know all the while that it does no such thing? Did Socrates really believe that the moon was something other than a stone? In the face of modern science, in the presence of nihilism, how does Scripture respond to these accusations that its wisdom is sophistry, that its justice masks the desire for revenge, that its appearance does not cloak reality, but the grandeur of a magnificent illusion?

The *kedoshim* will not tolerate an austere, moral humanism, one that would disassociate the word from the thing, for the word *dvar* connotes both word and thing. What of the relation between them? Here there is introduced a preliminary but primordial distinction between the mode of address, "the saying, and the thing said." The act of saying in the *kedoshim* repeats the thing said but amplifies the relations between the speaker and those addressed through the opening of the 'saying.'

The experience of overwhelming arbitrariness is contested in the intimacy of imperative discourse. The overpowering evidence of certitude exists between the holy one and the meaning of the people, Israel, who are called upon to become a "holy people." Restating the centrality of moral categories in an almost tabular correspondence with the *mishpatim*, justice now acts as a fence around the possible madness that can result from a direct contact with the sacred. In this divine gesture lies the absolution of dependence; the creator testifies to his grandeur by creating a being who can call him to account in the name of one of his attributes, the one which he most manifestly shares with his people, i.e. justice. Here, as in many other instances, we are reminded of the centrality of Abraham.

Justice itself is to be expressed in a manner which is holy. The pre-moral and the supra-moral are not left to preference, in the case of the former, or unjust faith, in the case of the latter. The created world is textured in its grossest materiality with sparks of holiness. There are things, actions, and words that fit together, and other things that do not belong together. There is a way to plow, a way to harvest, a way to dress, and a way to mourn. There is a way to love that serves justice, and a way to distance oneself from the spirit of revenge that inhibits the production of justice: "Surely you shall rebuke your neighbor so that you sin not on his account... You shall love your neightbor as yourself" (Lev. 19:17). To hallow the everyday, to sanctify the flesh of food that becomes the food of flesh, makes hope, and it makes certain what otherwise would become the invasive arbitrariness of daily experience.

The evidence of this certitude is in the saying: "you shall be holy, for I the Lord your God am holy." This refrain follows upon virtually every cluster of utterances. To become holy is the ultimate act of security from the affective mode of esthetic experience. It is integrity, righteousness, that commands upright conduct. Sanctifying the simplest tasks gives them beauty and symmetry. It is in this relation where the mine subordinates itself to the ours and the ours to the Yours that the power of the divine transforms the overpowering sense of arbitrariness into the overwhelming existence of holiness.

All egoism is divested, unmasked, disarmed. The relation of the infinite to the finite is asymmetrical. Through time and space, intimacy and relation are secured by enacting a visible existence where the interior sojourn is uprooted before the Other.

The Reason of all reasons is withheld. The assurance comes in the saying, in the welcoming of the face of the other. The holy relations with the other begin in the refusal to hold him hostage, where he would demonically belong to me, become my possession. For the stranger as well as the neighbor belongs to the absotutely 'other.' Ours is a relation that dwells profitably in mutual regard. I am answerable for him. This is my way of responding, of producing justice. I am answerable to him. This is sanctification of a love premised on justice that raises up and works at the completing of creation.

There is an installed order to creation. Man gives names to the animals. The beasts of burden that are permitted to be yoked together and those that are not, these beasts are not the products of human speech, and therefore retain a measure of dignity. Nor is the blood of flesh to be spilled easily let alone eaten without reservation: "for the life is in the blood." Fruit bearing trees cannot be plucked before the fruit matures. Eating from the knowledge of good and evil leaves the trees of the field intact and intractible. Even the artifacts, the creation of man's own hand, are not to be destroyed wantonly. And most certainly they are not to be worshipped.

There is an order to human relations, unions forbidden and permitted. All this serves the purpose of distancing the familiar, so that the familial relations may exist in holiness where the father is continued in the rupture of independence which is the son, so that the son will fear "everyman, his mother and his father," not out of affect or even obligation but because of reverence: "I the Lord your God am holy, therefore you shall be holy."

The naming of animals is given over to man. The holy itself is alone able to call darkness, 'night,' and light, 'day.' The sun rises and also sets because there was and is evening and morning, one day.

Hence, the petition of the psalmist: "Teach us to number our days that we may get us a heart of wisdom" (Psalm 90:12).

## NOTES

[1] See F. Rosenzweig, "The New Thinking" in *The Life and Thought of Frantz Rosenzweig*, tr. and ed. Nahum Glatzer (New York: Schocken, 1972).

[2] See Silvano Arieti, *Abraham and the Contemporary Mind* (New York: Basic Books, 1981), p. viii.

[3] See *Fear and Trembling* and *The Sickness unto Death*, tr. Walter Lowrie (New York: Anchor, 1954).

[4] See *Yalkut MeAm Lo'ez*, Vol. II, tr. A. Kaplan (New York: Maznaim, 1977), pp. 312-344.

[5] *MeAm Lo'ez*, p. 339.

[6] See R. Menachem M. Schneersohn, *Likkutei Sichot*, Vol. I: *Bereshis* (New York: Kehot Publication Society, 1982), pp. 82-122.

[7] *Likkutei Sichot.*

[8] As Rashi comments, the word *garti* has the numerical value 613, implying that while sojourning with the wicked Lavan, I have performed the 613 *mitvoth*. See Rashi, *The Pentateuch and Rashi's Commentaries*, 5 vol. (Philadelphia: Jewish Publication Society, 1949), p. 321. Except where otherwise noted, citations to Rashi, the most respected of Rabbinic commentators, are to this edition and are found beneath the Biblical text being used in this discussion.

[9] Rashi, p. 373.

[10] *The Living Torah*, tr. and commentary by Areyah Kaplan (New York: Maznaim Publishing, 1981), p. 110.

[11] *Tz'enah Ur'enah: The Classic Anthology of Torah Lore and Midrashic Comment*, tr. Miriam Stark Zakon (New York: Mesorah Publications, 1983), p. 200.

# The Bible

12 Kierkegaard, in the *Philosophic Fragments*, asks a question of Socrates. From a logical point of view this implies an infinite regress. Is there a teacher of all teachers? The Psalmist, even in the midst of his most radical questioning affirms that there is a teacher of all teachers: "Teach us to number our days that we may get us a heart of wisdom" (Psalm 90). There are several decise ways in which the Hebraic concept of knowledge differs from the concept of knowledge found in the Greek world.

13 Compare with Gen. 15:14, Gen. 17:21, 26:5, and Gen. 50:24.

14 Other commentators indicate that the sense of the statement is "I will be with you in other exiles as I have been with you in this one."

15 On Rosh Hashanna toil ceased and on the 15th of Nissan the outgoing from Egypt commenced. See *Tz'enah Ur'enah*, p. 335.

16 *Tz'enah Ur'enah*, p. 335.

17 *Tz'enah Ur'enah*, pp. 335-336.

18 And Moses, in a rare moment capturing the tone of the 90th Psalm brings the complaint of the people before God: "O Lord, why do You mistreat Your people? Why did You send me? As soon as I came to Pharaoh to speak in Your name, he made things worse for these people. You have done nothing to help your people" (Exodus 5:22). [According to some commetators Moses is rebuked for his lament: (*Tz'enah Ur'enah*, p. 334). He is, for example compared unfavorably to Abraham who rushed to God's bidding at the *Akedah*, the binding of Isaac.]

19 See Rashi, vol II, p. 62.

20 *The Living Torah*, p. 51.

21 It is Aaron and not Moses who struck the river, because the river is credited with the kindness of concealing Moses as an infant.

22 *The Living Torah*, p. 50.

[23]*Tz'enah Ur'enah*, pp. 347-348.

[24]Targener Yonathon, *Mekhilta*, see *The Living Torah*, p. 175.

[25]*The Living Torah*, p. 515.

[26]*The Living Torah* , p. 175.

[27]*Tz'enah Ur'enah*, p. 395.

[28]*Tz'enah Ur'enah*, p. 395.

[29]*The Living Torah*, p. 110.

[30]*Tz'enah Ur'enah*, p. 349.

[31]*Tz'enah Ur'enah*, p. 350.

[32]Abraham Chill, *The Mitzvots* (New York: Bloch Publishing, 1974), p. 19.

[33]Friederich Nietzsche, *Thus Spoke Zarathustra* in *The Viking Portable Nietzsche*, tr. and ed. Walter Kaufman (New York: Viking, 1968), p. 211.

[34]*Midrash Rabba Vayikra* (Leviticus), tr. J. Slotki (London: Soncino, 1939).

# Suggested Readings on the Bible

A representative sampling of the Biblical material includes readings from the three primary divisions of the Hebraic Bible. The commentary literature is vital to enabling the student to grasp the multiple levels of meaning in the text. A brief list of commentary literature follows: this table of suggested readings from the Bible.

**Torah:**

Genesis - Entire Book
Exodus - Chapters 1-25; 31-35
Leviticus - Chapters 1-6; 16; 25
Numbers - Chapters 10-36
Deuteronomy - Entire Book

**Prophets:**

Samuel I, II
Amos
Jonah
Hosea

**Writings:**

Book of Psalms
Job
Ecclesiastes
Chronicles

**Bibliography:**

*The Living Torah: The Five Books of Moses* , tr. and ed.Rabbi Areyeh Kaplan (New York: Maznaim Publishing Co., 1981).

> A new translation based on traditional Jewish sources with notes, introduction, maps, tables, charts, bibliography, and index. The most idiomatic translation of the Five Books of Moses from Hebrew into English. The Kaplan translation is a monumental achievement of scholarship, which has the advantages of clearly outlining the contents of the text as

well as interpolating the commentary tradition within the body of the text. Moreover, the footnotes provide an accurate, valuable, although very terse amplification of textual ambiguities, drawing on hundreds of commentaries. At times the poetic sensibility of Scripture is sacrificed for the sake of accuracy in translation.

*The Holy Scriptures* (Philadelphia: Jewish Publication Society of America, 1955).

The translation is according to the Masoretic text and includes the entire Hebrew Bible.

Menachem M. Schneerson, *Likkutei Sichot,* Vol. I, II, tr. from Yiddish by J. Immanuel Schochet (New York: Kehot Publication Society, 1980).

An anthology of talks by the Lubavitcher Rebbe. Magnificent commentaries on the Torah, arranged systematically by the greatest contemporary Chassidic commentator. The discourses open the reader to the mystical dimension of text (*sod*) as well as clarifying the plain sense of text (*pshat*), revealing allusions (*remez*), and the moral aspects (*derush*). These four levels of *Pshat, Remez, Dreush,* and *Sod* (*PaRDeS*) are uncovered severally and in their interelation.

Rashi (acronym for Rabbi Shlomo ben Yitschak) (1040-1105). Commentator on Scripture and Talmud *par excellence.* Rashi's commentaries are found in all major Rabbinical compilations. While the language of Rashi's commentaries tends to be spare, the insights and lucidity of expression make his observations invaluable. The aid of his commentaries is to elucidate the oral, Rabbinic reading of essential Biblical and Rabbinic texts. The emphasis is on the phenomenological aspects of the text, i.e., to make sense out of the most manifest content provided by the text, taking the plain surface (*pshat*) of the text as signifying what it apparently says except as otherwise given.

There are two English editions of Rashi each of which are valuable for the non-Hebrew speaking reader. These are:

184

# The Bible

*The Pentateuch and Rashi's Commentary: A Linear Translation into English*, 5 vol., tr. Rabbi Abraham ben Isiah and Rabbi Benjamin Sharfman. (Philadelphia: S.S. & R Publishing Co., Inc., Press of the Jewish Publication Society, 1949).

These volumes are chronological, bi-lingual exposition of the Pentateuch with Rashi's commentary of individual words and phrases at the bottom of each page. The words or phrases from the Pentateuch are highlighted before introducing the commentary. The complete Pentateuch is presented in Hebrew and English by phrases or words to which the commentary is keyed.

*Pentateuch with Rashi's Commentary*, 5 vol.,tr. Rosenbaum and A. M. Silberman (New York:  Hebrew Publishing Co.)..

Provides a more thematic, running commentary by Rashi. This collection, often referred to as the "Silberman" edition is perhaps a bit easier for the somewhat more advanced student. Reference to Hebrew is occasionally assumed. The commentary is somewhat more extended. In addition, the collection includes the Aramaic translation (not translated into English) of *Targum Onkelos*. This Aramaic translation (ca. 90 C.E.) tends to render the text homiletically rather than literally.

*Tz'enah Ur'enah*, compiled by Rabbi Yaakov ben Yitzchak Askenazi, 3 vol., tr. from Yiddish by Miriam Stark Zakon (New York: Mesorah Publications, Ltd. 1983).

The exact date and place of the original publication remains uncertain, ranging from Prague in 1608 to Basle, 1622. The title means "Come Out and See" (Song of Songs, 3:11). The *Tz'enah Ur'enah* appears in English in 3 vols. The source material is drawn from various midrashic (non-legalistic) sources. In addition to amplifying Rashi's commentary, the text draws heavily on Bachya by Asher (1263-1340). Bachya is a major Torah commentator and philosopher. The *Tz'enah Ur'enah* is the most widely read and translated (over 210 editions) of all Yiddish commentaries on Torah. It is rich in illustrative material stressing both the metaphorical and moral dimensions of the Torah.

*MeAm Lo'ez* -published as *The Torah Anthology*, 14 vol.,tr. by Rabbi Areyeh Kaplan (New York: Maznaim Publishing Co., 1977).

A narrative, running commentary on the Torah originally written in Ladino (Judeo-Spanish) by Rabbi Yaakov Culi (1689-1732), first published in Constantinople, 1730-33, the *Yalkut MeAm Lo'ez*, a Hebrew translation by Rabbi Shmuel Yerushalmi was published in Jerusalem, 1967-71. The text draws on Talmudic and Midrashic sources and provides a compendious and lucid treatment of the Torah. Among Sephardic (Oriental) Jewry the *MeAm Lo'ez* has a status that is comparable to that of Rashi.

# APPENDIX ON THE BIBLE

## 1. The Bible and Hermeneutics

What follows is a brief exposition of the divisions and interpretation of the Biblical text according to the traditions of Rabbinic Judaism. While this material does not always reflect the views of contemporary rationalistic Biblical criticism, it does give some insight into the Rabbinic Biblical concept of redaction and hermenueutics. The continuity and rigor of Rabbinic interpretations of the Biblical texts remains one of the most powerful of all the intellectual traditions of the West. This subject, of course, deserves separate and serious consaideration in a more extensive context.

According to Rabbinic Judaism, Torah in its most restrictive sense refers to the first five books of the Hebraic Bible. These include: Genesis (*Bereshis*), Exodus (*Shemos*), Leviticus (*Vayikra*), Numbers (*Bramidbar*), and Deuteronomy (*Devarim*). The Hebrew word 'Torah' derives from the Hebrew root word for instruction (*Ho'rah*). It is used to signify teaching or way. When it is noted that Psalm 90 is the only fragment ascribed to Moses outside of the written text of the five books, and that this holds true of the Hebraic Bible in its entirety, we are referring only to the written text that begins with Genesis and ends with Chronicles. The acronym deriving from the three major portions of the Hebraic Bible is *Tanak*: *Tanak* refers to Torah proper, the writings of the Prophets (*Nevi'im*), and the 'writings' or *Kesuvim*. It is a fundamental tenet of normative Judaism that the every word of the first five books was divinely authored and written down by Moses.

The Prophets technically begin with the Book of Joshua (*Yehoshua*) and conclude with the words of Malachi. Altogether there are eight books in the *Nevi'im* including: 1.) Joshua (*Yeshua*); 2.) Judges (*Shoftim*); 3.)Samuel (1+2) (*Shmuel*); 4.) Kings (1+2) (*Melkhim*); 5.) Isaiah (*Yishiahu*); 6.) Jeremiah (*Yirmiahu*); 7.) Ezekiel

(*Yechezkel*); 8.) The Twelve (*Trey Asar*) refer to the twelve 'Minor' Prophets, called 'minor' only because their writings are more condensed. The Twelve are: 1.) Hosea (*Hoshea*); 2.) Joel (*Yoel*); 3.) ; Amos; 4.) Obadiah; 5.) Jonah (*Yonah*); 6.) Micah (*Mikhah*); 7.) Nahum (*Nachum*); 8.) Habbakkuk; 9.) Zephanaiah; 10.) Haggai; 11.) Zachariah; 12.) Malachi. The Prophets are bound by the instruction and commandments of Torah and cannot contradict, therefore, any portion of the Torah. It is through prophetic vision that the books of *Nevi'im* are held to have been composed according to normative Judaism. The central function of the prophets is to remind, encourage, and admonish the people to keep the words of the Torah with the urgency of moral passions pressed by the 'letter' of the Law of Torah.

The most familiar portion of the *Tanak* to contemporary readers are the eleven books of the *Kesuvim* (writings). Beginning with 1. Psalms (*Tehillim*) and including: 2. Proverbs (*Mishley*); 3. Job (*Iyyou*) 4. Song of Songs (*Shir HaShirim*); 5. Ruth (*Rus* 1); 6. Lamentations (*Eikah*); 7. Ecclesiastes (*Koheles*); 8. Esther; 9. Daniel; 10. Ezra and Nehemiah; 11. Chronicles (1+2) (*Divrey HaYamim*). The Eleven books of the Kesuvim have various functions ranging from the centrality of Prayer in Psalms to the recounting of central events and the geneology of Biblical history in Chronicles. While not a totality, each text presents a certain perspective of the Biblical world expressive of the emotional, passional life of Biblical existence. The consolation writings are held to be the product of divine inspiration where the author is not compelled by prophetic trance or vision and without necessarily being able to explain the source of his moral vision, and therefore, without the binding self-referential authority or responsibility incumbent on the prophets.

There are the twenty-four books of the *Tanak*: the five books of the Torah, the eight books of the prophets, and the eleven books of writings. The level of Divine Inspiration (*Ruach Nevuah*), which most sympathetic readers of the text from a Humanistic standpoint are inclined to credit the Bible, is from a Rabbinic standpoint the least of the three levels in terms of ultimate meaning when compared to the status of prophetic and Mosaic claims.

The final reduction or compilation of the written text (*Mikra*) was completed by Ezra the Scribe and Prophet in conjunction with the Great Assembly (*Knessess Ha Gedolah*). This occured just after the end of the Babylonian exile, ca. 353 B.C.E. From that time the Mikra or written text of *Tanak* could not be altered by addition or deletion.

This discussion is further amplified in the *Gemara* (the root word *gamar* means to study and to finish). The Gemara paralleling the same portions or *Mishnah*, in fact restate the *Mishnah* in its entirety, and then sets out detailed analysis of the problems related to understanding and applying the *Halakah* (Law) of the *Mishnah*. For the ensuing three hundred years after the compilation of the *Mishnah*, the analysis and conclusion of the *Mishnah* were refined. In 505 B.C.E. the *Mishnah* now circumscribed by the Gemara was published as the Babylonian Talmud. The status of the Babylonian Talmud, which contains 37 tracts of the 63 portions of the *Mishnah* has a definitive status within normative Judaism: "The Babylonian Talmud was accepted by all Israel as the final binding authority in all questions of religion and law. All subsequent codifications of Torah law are binding only insofar as they are based on the Talmud."[1]

## 2. Hermeneutics

Since the Hebraic Bible is sacred, even if in varying degrees of authority, to Christianity and Islam, as well as Judaism, it is essentially and decisively the oral Torah which distinguishes the normative, Jewish reading of the text. Since Christianity and Islam have superceding texts, the New Testament, and the Koran, respectively, the theory and principle of interpretation guiding the understanding of the text remains a matter of ultimate importance to Judaism. Still, while the written Torah has consequences unique to the practice of Judaism which has no superceding text, what is critical in grasping the category of the oral Torah, the concept of interpretation, what Biblical scholars today prefer to call hermeneutics, has universal implications.

As a 17th century Rabbinic commentary, the *MeAm Lo' ez* puts it:

> Moses received the Torah from the One who revealed himself at Sinai. As God taught Moses each commandment, He also taught him all the points which are indispensible to the observance of the commandments. The written Torah is extremely concise, and is often abstract. Therefore, it is difficult to understand any passage without knowing the interpretation in the oral Torah.[2]

In matters of *Halakah* or Law, the interpretation is indispensible to its application. This is true even of words written on the tablet, the Ten Commandments: "Remember the Sabbath Day to keep it holy." How shall it be made holy? What is to be done, what is not to be done? No work shall be done. What constitutes work? Similarly, take the case of a prohibiting commandment: "Thou shalt not murder." Does the text indicate pure pacifism or is there room for self defense? What constitutes self-defense? Is it ever obligatory to defend oneself in the most terrible way? All of these questions bring home to us the central need for interpretation.

Just as the written Torah was received by Moses at Sinai, and was transmitted to the Men of Great Assembly through the Elders and Prophets, so too was the oral Torah. The meaning of Torah itself as a word-concept becomes more expansive, to include not only all of the written Tanak but also the illumination and deliberation of the transmitters of the text. The Great Assembly, or Sanhedrin of one hundred twenty exemplary scholars, led by Ezra at the time of the beginning of the Second Temple, undertook to codify much of the Oral Torah in a form that could be memorized by the students. This codification was set down in its most precise form by Rabbi Yehudah the Prince in 188 C.E. "One reason for this name, *Mishnah*, was that it was meant to be reviewed (*Shanah*) over and over until memorized."3

The opening chapter of the first book of the Six Tractates which comprise the *Mishnah* begins with a consideration that appears as complex as oral tradition itself. "From when onwards are we to read the *Shema* in the evening?" The reciting of the *Shema* drawn from these Biblical sources (Deut. 6, 4-9; Deut. 11, 13-21; Numbers 15, 37-41) is the central liturgical affirmation of Jewish Faith. It begins: "Hear, O Israel, the Lord is ours, the Lord is One." The unity God (the very essence of monotheism) is bound together with the oneness of Israel, and therefore implicitly with the unity of the human self. The *Shema* is to be proclaimed twice daily, morning and evening. When does the evening end and when does the morning begin? This is precisely the matter deliberated on: Until the end of First watch (the night being divided into three watches) or until midnight or until dawn? Until dawn as the sages say. (However, it is better to do so before midnight, in order to keep a man from transgression.) This is the first fence built around the Torah. But, what really after all is dawn and how can the matter be known? The second chapter of the *Mishnah* begins by asking: "At what time does one begin to recite the Shema in morning?" When one can distinguish blue and R. Eliezer says, "Between blue and green" (and concludes it) by sunrise. This discussion is not as archane as it might appear, especially when one considers the prayer of the Psalmist: "Teach us to number our days that we may get us a heart of wisdom." To number our days we must be able to determine minimally the unity of a single day. The unity of day depends on the relation of light and darkness to what we call 'day' and 'night.' And it is this matter that is taken up straight away in the beginning of the Book of Beginnings, Genesis.

The remarkable aspect of the Rabbinic theory of interpretation is that through the Oral Torah, the Bible is provided with a hermeneutic- -a way of interpretation intrinsic to its understanding, explanation, and expansion. This is unique within the Western religious tradition, and in fact appears to have no parallel within the other religions of the world, ancient or modern, Western or Eastern. It is, then, appropriate to call Israel, the people of the Book.

## 3. On Rationalistic Biblical Criticism and the Tetragreammaton

It is noteworthy to mention that the Rabbinic tradition was not unaware of the interpretive complexities posed by the different names used to refer to God. The process of 'de-mystifying' the Bible launched by Spinoza in the 17th century aimed at purging the text of every element that was, by the standards of the Enlightenment neither rational nor objective. In the 19th century Julius Welhausen and his disciples in the school of 'higher' Biblical criticism made what was regarded as a 'momentous discovery.' Amid the many contradictions in the text were different names used to refer to God beginning with the first two chapters of Genesis. While the name *Elokhim* is used in the first chapter, the Tetragrammaton is used in the second. From this observation was derived the hypothesis that different literary strata could be located in the text. Wherever the name Elokhim is used the author(s) was characterized as the "E" writer. Where the Tetragrammaton is employed, the "author" became known as the "J" writer. Refinements were introduced. The Book of Deuteronomy was ascribed, presumably because of its variances with the earlier four books as the "D" writer. A 'science' of the text continuing to the present day emerged as dominant within literary criticism. Linguistic evidence, archaeological data, antiquarian history all were used in the serve of explicating the text. The Bible, according to this view, was written by a committee over a long period of time, governed by the customs, needs and institutions of the times.

Was God, then, mistaken when he implied that He was telling Moses something emphatically new when He said to Moses: "You must (then) say to the Israelites, 'YHVH', the God of your fathers, the God of Abraham, Isaac and Jacob, sent me to you. This is my eternal name, and this is how I am to be recalled for all generations" (Ex. 3:15). The issue is made even more puzzling and precise when: "God spoke to Moses and said to him, 'I am YHVH. I revealed Myself to Abraham, Isaac and Jacob as God Almighty [*El Shad dai*] and did not allow them to know Me by My name YHVH'" (Exodus 6:2). The Bible uses the Tetragrammaton in speaking to Abraham (Genesis 15:7) and Jacob (Genesis 28:13). Moreover, as A. Kaplan points out the Tetragrammaton was never used in speech before the time of the Patriarchs. Among the Patriarchs, the Tetragrammaton was known, but not its inner significance (Ramban; Ibn Ezra).[4] In numerous places, as Kaplan notes, the Patriarchs used the name themselves, the angels in several places, and even non-Hebrews. Kaplan citing Maimonides' *Guide for the Perplexed* and other sources remarks:

> This was because the Patriarchs received their prophecy from the level associated with the name El Shaddai; while only Moses received it from the level associated with the Tetragammaton. (cf. *Moreh Nexukim* 2:35)

It is, therefore, appropriate that the encounter by the bush that burns, but does not consume itself, is at the same time the occasion for the revelation to Moses of the Tetragrammaton, the four letter name of God. Even the closest approximate transliterations are inexact and, from a Rabbinic perspective, inappropriate if not altogether forbidden. It may not be pronounced under any circumstances (Sanhedrin). It is this name that denotes God's utter transcendance according to Maimonides (*Guide for the Perplexed* 1.61) and Judah Ha Levi (*Kuzari* 2.2). As Areyeh Kaplan notes, "God is telling Moses that not only is the initial purpose of creation now being fulfilled, but also the process that will insure its continual existence."[5] [When read aloud in English translation, it is this name that is refered to by the word "Lord." The various Rabbinic appelations are *Ha Shem* (the name) or

YHVH, rendering an approximation of the four Hebrew letters--Yudi, Hay, Vav, I--which has the virtue of making the name unpronounceable. Also the inversion Havye is commonly used for purposes of study. In the Kabbalistic literature YHVH is associated with the attribute of *Chesed* (mercy or kindness).]

# Bible Appendix

## NOTES

[1]*The Living Torah*, tr. and commentary by Areyah Kaplan (New York: Maznaim, 1981), p. 191.

[2]*MeAm Lo'ez*, Vol. II, tr. Areyah Kaplan (New York: Maznaim, 1977), p. 13.

[3]Areyah Kaplan, *Handbook of Jewish Thought* (New York: Maznaim, 1978), pp. 185-189.

[4] *The Living Torah*, p. 157

[5]*The Living Torah*, p. 152.

Chapter Seven

# EPILOGUE:
# KNOWLEDGE AND EXISTENCE

## I. Nature and Time

From the perspective of the modern world we look back towards our beginnings in our own search for self-understanding. In this book we have argued that the essential roots of human identity in the Western tradition, however diffused and reimagined during the progress of history, are to be found in the literary and philosophic texts of ancient Greece and in the religious-existential world of the Bible. If we look from the perspective of contemporary modernity, we can see two strikingly different processes at work in these traditions.

In the Greek tradition we find a sequence of authors and texts that reach from Homer to Aristotle and an evolution toward a dominant rationalism. Within this tradition we find a remarkable variety of kinds of text--epic, tragedy, philosophic dialogue, philosophic treatise. Each text contains its own individual complexity and serves as a model for future ages. Homer both embodies the epic of war and survivial and presents the fundamental mode of narrative that extends into modern fiction. Among our chosen authors and texts, however, we can see a striking development within the Greek tradition, a development that had the most profound impact on the evolution of the West. This is, of course, the ascendancy of reason as the progressive answer to the latent oppositions within human nature. Homer portrays the pathos, fear, grandeur, and failure of the Greek heroic ethic in *The Iliad*. But along with his portrayal of the public fortunes of war and honor, Homer addresses the mysteries of human fate and mortality. The unparalleled magnificence of the concluding episode of *The Iliad* establishes a profound understanding of the price of being human. The scene of Achilles and Priam as they meet over the body of Hector reaches a level of pathos and tragic significance that reveals the fullness of embodied existence. The agonistic opposition of warriors resolves in Book XXIV of *The Iliad* into the shared understanding of Priam and Achilles about the tragic sorrow of human existence.

The great Greek tragedians, especially Aeschylus and Sophocles, share in Homer's sense of human grandeur and limit in suffering. Sophocles particularly understands the human drive to know even in the face of terrible opposition, and Oedipus becomes a model of tragic self-knowledge that is inextricably bound up with suffering. Homer and the tragedians share in the sense of the heroic possiblity of human beings and the power that nature thrusts against them. In the natural ethic of the Homeric world human beings find embodied existence-- Achilles' grief over the slain Patroklus, Odysseus' mastery over his own bow and the belligerent suitors--but they cannot transcend the imposed boundaries of the natural world. Along with the joy of existence and the sharp grief over mortality, the Homeric world betrays a sense of melancholy that the concentrated forces of muscle and mind are ultimately bounded by the immovable reality of physical nature. The horizon of "the barren salt sea" surrounds even the triumphant Odysseus as he reclaims his identity and kingship in Ithaca.

Within the ancient Greek world, what we have called "the turn toward reason" marks a radical shift in the development of the West. The images and actions set forth by Homer and the tragedians give way to the dialectical inquiry of Socrates and Plato, and the analytic method of Aristotle. The gain in power of the turn toward reason results in the systematization that reaches such consummate heights in Aristotle. But a significant human price is paid for the power and aloofness of analytical reasoning. As we see even in the *Symposium*, the dialectical investigation of eros leads not toward but away from persons. If we take Socrates' pivotal speech as the intended pinnacle of the dialogue, then we see that the idea of absolute beauty, as revealed by Diotima to Socrates, supplants the actuality of specific relationship championed by young Phaedrus. In the view of Socrates this turn toward absolute beauty fosters proper philosophic activity. The gain for philosophy is great, but the price in terms of human relations must give one pause.

Standing in latent opposition to the world of the Greeks is the world of the Hebraic Bible. Here existence takes part in a dynamic that includes but is not exclusively bounded by nature. The idea of creation that sets its seal on the opening of the Bible is completely missing from the Greek world. As a consequence, the Biblical horizon extends not just to the edge of the salt sea but towards infinity. And just as creation presents an infinite horizon to humans, so it also intiates the root ideas of beginnings, change, and time. With the exodus from Egypt forming the great historical center to the events of the five books of Moses, the Bible sets forth a vision of human existence that, while able to contemplate the infinite horizon, rests upon the ground of time, history, and personal immediacy. This immediacy is charged by divine concern and by the imperative of the exigencies and the promise of time. Thus, Abraham sets out from Ur toward a homeland of renewed existence, never before known to him. The Israelites overthrow the yoke of tyranny and step forward in time and space toward both the encounter with the divine and their own historical awareness. The Biblical dynamic of existence establishes the concepts of time, history, and person that remain at the heart of Western thinking about self-knowledge.

RECLAIMING THE HUMANITIES

## II.  Self-Knowledge and Reason

The question which dominates our inquiry is human existence reflected to thought in its beginnings. The 'Humanities' as a subject of study presupposes this human subject, before all abstractions of a 'subject matter.'  What is reflected to thought is embodied in this seminal literature, which is itself an inscribed reflection of human subjects that remain enduring images through changing historical conditions.  There is a constant tension between 'distance' and 'relation' that compells us to distinguish images of ourselves from those of the thinkers and texts with whom we would engage in dialogue. The closer we come to the beginnings of this subject matter, the more acutely we see differences of outlook within contexts that from a distance appear indistinguishable.

The distance from Homer to Aristotle, measured by perspective as opposed to chronology, is perhaps greater that the distance from Aristotle to the present. This view was first advanced by Nietzsche in *The Birth of Tragedy*. In fact we do see a progressive rationalizing of existence, which we as the children of the Enlightenment are apt to view as the 'progress' of civilization.

Such progress is qualified when we realize that the turn toward reason submerges the sense of immediate experience familiar to the Homeric subject.  Self-certainty, as is evident from the flicker of philosophic consciousness in Achilles, clouds the tragic sensibility so exquisitely described by Aeschylus and Sophocles.  Even from the time of Aeschylus to that of Sophocles, as we move through the heart of Greek tragedy, the refining of moral sensibilities prefigures the inseparable connection between self-knowledge and right conduct. Oedipus as depicted by Sophocles is as different from Prometheus as is Prometheus from Odysseus.

Viewed from the perspective of Aristotle's discussion of human freedom, Odysseus deliberates not about the ends of action, but the means of achieving an end, i.e, what is recognized by the Greek heroes to be estimable. The opposition between gods and mortals, nature and society, power and moral excellecne, is laid bare by Aeschylus in a way that is partially concealed by Homer. The plastic forms of the epic change dramatically. The tension between natural force and human understanding is exposed as an irresolvable opposition. Existence reflected to thought loosens the intimacy and violent innocence that is the elixir of Homeric man. Prometheus becomes more nearly our contemporary than Aristotle in this respect. The Socratic-Platonic equation of 'wisdom equals excellence equals happiness' does not always appear to work. This distance between subject and self-knowledge derives here from a silent, menacing cosmos.

In Oedipus, as we have seen, suffering is the purchase price of self-knowledge. The self-reflective subject who would rule cities is confronted by the task of mastering the citadel of his own identity and latent personal destiny. Blinding self-recognition is inapprorpiate for the validictory rhetoric that is the hall mark of graduation from the liberal arts. For Sophocles the fault, however, is not in the stars but in ourselves. Even Camus is forced to conclude, reflecting on the *Antigone*, that for Oedipus at the end: 'All is well.' For Oedipus the logic of the Socratic-Platonic equation remains to be discovered.

The rule of *logos* in the thought of the Platonic Socrates effects a fundamental change in the relation of existence to thematization and thus initiates a shift from a narrative or dramatic view of existence to a more abstract and detached perspective on human nature. The Platonic project subordinates the thinker to his thoughts through just and rational discourse. The human subject is not forced to re-invent the world into which he is born. Rather, such inquiry leads toward systematic thinking. What remains unchanging in all changing circumstances is elevated to the level of systematic thinking that, while elicited in the presence of a teacher, aims at providing the learner with an independent attachment to the *eide* whose shapes remain essentially the same. A political philosophy inevitably results from the always implicit concern to establish a just city, safe guarded for the task of philosophy.

The apology of the Socratic inquiry does not perish with the verdict rendered by the the jury that finds him guilty and sentences him to death. Rather, in the hands of Plato the struggle between excellence and power, imaged as early as the feud between Achilles and Agamemnon by Homer in *The Iliad*, becomes a subject for systematic reflection. When Socrates asks the polititians about their purported wisdom in the *Apology*, he establishes the fact that power does not assure wisdom. For the subject who desires happiness must know what happiness is. This means that he must undertake the path to self-knowledge. Self-knowledge takes place within a context, which for Plato is the polis.

In the *Republic* Plato presents a search for the just city that explores almost every possible form or government. Even the tyrant who rules in accordance with his own interests and desires is subject to the limitation that, in not knowing what is best for him, he may be charting a course to unhappiness and injustice as well as his own downfall. Power becomes authority in the city only when it is just. It is just proportion raised to the philosophic level of understanding of what is inherently excellent. What is inherently excellent in all its various appearances is reflected through a seeing that perpetually corrects itself through the work of dialectical thinking. Such thinking is clothed in the form of dialogue.

The form of dialogue stands in relation to its content in much the same way that experience does to idea. The agonistic impulse which impells the struggle of the Homeric warrior is sublimated in the wrestling match that dwells within the realm of dialectical discourse. The understanding of Plato involves study on the part of the reader, who himself becomes, through the medium of the dialogues, a student of Socrates.

In this advance of reason, which culminates in the thought of Aristotle, a quiet but decisive division of knowledge and existence takes place. Plato initiates in his dialogues the quest for systematic understanding that Aristotle perfects. Aristotle proceeds by the method of division and analysis. This permits a greater distance for surveying the data of the cosmos inhabited by the human subject. The collating, indexing, and ordering of the cosmos becomes the standard method against which all subsequent reflection on the natural world is measured until the time of the Enlightenment.

With Aristotle, the disciplinary study of the human subject commences. Philosophy, for instance, is divided by Aristotle for the purpose of its study into its many branches. Logic becomes for him, as it is for us, the science of statements. Ethics is concerned with right conduct. Metaphysics is a separate branch of philosophic study concerned with first principles and primary causes. The subtlety of the *Symposium* is displaced by the *Poetics* of Aristotle and its logical, structured categories. The features of tragedy are described and codified in this first tract of literary criticism. The relations of logic to metaphysics become uncertain. Each subject matter is studied in external relation to every other. The human subject beneath the disciplinary constructs is a series of profiles that becomes a portrait only in the minds of other thinkers. One must look to specialists for self-knowledge as well as knowledge of the world.

Under the view of this ordering of the world, Homer and the tragedians become pre-philosophical. Until our own times, this view has prejudiced most serious readers. Declarative discourse becomes under the reign of reason the model of reflective philosophical understanding. The dramatic form of the dialogue is too textured, too ambiguous to be of use for the purpose of knowledge that is reliable and capable of producing stable results. Hence, the one I would enounter in the polis can carry on his metaphysical reflections without my questioning. In turn, the life of the polis is too exigent to be preoccupied with questions that belong properly to logic and metaphysics. This disintegrating of the human subject beneath such reflections reults in pervasivie fragmentation. As long as there is a generally shared, easy sense of what is real, then there is no essential need to rethink pedagogy. This is plain from the opening lines of Aristotle's *Ethics*, where goods are described as corresponding to ends and everything, whether craft, decision, investigation, or action, aims at diverse but given ends.

Maimonides, Thomas Aquinas, and Averroes explain Judaism, Christianity, and Islam respectively with constant reference to Aristotle, despite the distance of more than 1400 years. In the realm of ethics, Aristotle's views are not seriously challenged until the time of Kant's moral philosophy in the late eighteenth century. This substitution of 'morality' for 'ethics' is itself the result of the scientific revolution. The inner world of Kant's categorical imperative needs to be secured only when the laws of the physical universe are overdetermined to such an extent that the cosmos as ordered by Aristotle becomes a Newtonian machine. Aristotle's logic persists until the twentieth century.

The crisis for both pedagogy and philosophic reflection arises when these goods, which express themselves as divers ends, are no longer self-evident. Then purpose and happiness become problematic for the living, human subject, for the subject has become problematic to himself. Nihilism becomes the extreme expression of a human subject that discovers himself to be inhabiting a world that does not claim him in the immediacy of his existence. The goods that express themselves as ends are experienced by the dispalced subject as aimless, relative, and arbitrary. The question of becoming human is overladen with pedagogy that assumes that the answers preempt our questions. Such radical questioning as exists for time-bound beings begs for urgent responses. Such responses are, however, dominated by the need for immediate practical application. Just in this experience of emergency lies the appeal of resolutions at the level of *techne*, a manipulating of circumstances, of data. Here, there is an experienced sense of the insufficiency of knowlege framed by a horizon of Totality. Encyclopedic knowledge will not by itself produce a purposeful, happy human being.

## III. Self-Knowledge and Promise

What a rethinking of our way back to the Biblical world promises is a different set of questions and a different range of understanding. The encounter between the world of Aristotle and the Biblical world is the unspoken reclaiming of the beginning of Western self-understanding. The hardess of philosophy and the consolation of religion move unknowlingly into the present historical hour. This, despite all precedents, Maimonides and Thomas Aquinas not withstanding. Here, it would be foolish not to recognize that these worlds, for the most part, appear in antiquity to be hermetically sealed off from one another. The legacy of the Hebraic Bible, however, continues in our own time through the resurgence of the three normative religions that have dominated and produced, through historical confluence or antigonism to political epochs, the spiritual legacy of the West.

The approaches to the Bible open to us are many. If *The Iliad* is the Bible of the Greeks, then we are certainly not free from encountering the Bible which produced the enduring religious tradition in the West. The way of the Biblical subject is opened for reflection by the recognition that the Bible not only has a sedimented history but that it is the source of our understanding of time and history for human self-knowldge. Within the context of reclaiming the humanities, we begin to catch sight of this human subject in the Biblical world. Here, we do not find systematic capturing of existence through thematization and reason. Rather, for the Biblical understanding of human subject, experience outstrips the thought we have about it. Without nostaglia or theology, the patterns of this world can be delineated.

What is perhaps most astonishing about the Biblical world is that, long before the emergence of existentialism in the nineteenth century, there is an overwhelming concern with activity and meaning of everyday life. Consider how much of the Book of Genesis is concerned with food and faminine, human children and the refusal to subordinate human progeny for an idea or for a wisdom that is disembodied. The high point in the life of Abraham concerns the divine command to bind Isaac, the son for whom he waited a life time, the son whom he loves. Contrast with this glorious image, Plato's narration of the death scene of Socrates in the *Phaedo*. The nameless sons of Socrates are ushered out of his presence, at his insistence, along with his wife, in order to make room for what is a higher reality, discoursing on the subject of philosophy.

The Biblical Jacob spends twenty years in exile, just as does Odysseus. Each is equipped with prudence, cunning, and strength. The wily Odysseus wrestles with men and nature and prevails, returning home to become again king over Ithaca. The movement from innocence to experience culminates in the triumphant re-assumption of a given identity in the midst of all alterations. Even Odysseus remains essentially the same, although self-knowledge has been added to his identity. Odysseus as giver and receiver of pain retains the root meaning of his name: "Zeus, why do you odysseus Odysseus so much?" (Book 1).

# Knowledge and Existence

Jacob struggles from the time of his birth. Altogether human, he labors in exile as an exploited herdsman, who is smitten by the frost in winter and the heat in summer. He wrestles with an angel of God and prevails. He is to be called Israel, the one who struggles with God. The change of name signifies a fundamental change in spiritual identity. Becoming outstrips adventure or philosophy in the Biblical world. The way of Jacob is through the world, not over it. Fatigued by daily happenings, the years of Jacob's life are measured out in terms of promisde rather than power. For Jacob, domesticity means establishing a home, not only finding the way back home: "And he built an altar and called the place El-beth-El [the house of God in the presence of God]" (Gen. 35:7). In response to Pharaoh's question about his age, Jacob replies ironically: "The days of my life have been few and bitter and have not equaled those of my fathers."

It is in the essential relation with the Infinite that the Biblical world of promise is formed. The absolutely Other stirs a restlessness toward perfection that remains to be achieved. Purpose governs the possibility of happiness. Both purpose and happiness are included within the Biblical horizon of promise. The end is not given by nature, but rather created by a transcendental God. Here, from the outset, the claim that there is a Teacher of all teachers must be taken earnestly. From the earliest passages of Genesis through the oppression and redemption from bondage in Egypt that dominates subsequent Israelite history, choice governs the way to happiness.

The primary metaphor of the human subject in the Biblical world is one of the journeying of the self toward the Other. This bond between self and Other we situate in the promise which both opens and binds word to deed and past to present and future. Time, then, becomes the inner horizon of Biblical existence and life in the West. 'Purpose,' in the Aristotelian, sense is a subject of reflection for Biblical man long before it emerges in Greek philosophy. As such, the patterns of human finitude are more visible in the the ever changing situation of Biblical persons than in the Greek fixity of character in the face of the inexorable cosmos. It is in this sense that the immutable truths of the Greek world stand in latent opposition to the Biblical dynamics of existence.

## IV. Knowledge and Existence: The Goals of a Humanistic Education

For the ancient Greeks, stretching from Homer to Aristotle, the odyssey of human understanding rises to the pursuit of wisdom, *sophia*. It is this discipline which we call philosophy. It differs from sophistry in this fundamental respect: sophistry aims at persuasive speech, where the objective is to make the opinion of the speaker prevail over that of his audience. Philosophy, on the other hand, aims at persuading oneself, in the presence of others, of truth that can be known. The failure of Athenian democracy to distinguish the philosophic pursuit of Socrates from the rhetorical, political project of the Sophists served only to immortalize the Socratic endeavor. For Plato the perfection of Socrates was never in question. Reason triumphs over death through courageous inquiry in the face of force, opposition, confusion, and ignorance.

To understand ourselves requires that we re-engage not only with the tragic-philosophic tradition of the Greeks, but with the Biblical-prohetic tradition as well. For the existence of knowledge is not reducible to the knowledge of existence. Finite human beings do not dwell in the motionless space habitable for Greek divinities. Time, rather than space, is the horizon in which Biblical man lives out his life, fatigued by the sweat of his labor that brings forth bread.

The outgoing from Egypt offers a different foundational metaphor for human existence from the one which we find in *The Odyssey*. It is a journey that ventures out of the self into a history

# Knowledge and Existence

where the future can be more perfect than the past. The Western concept of history as we know it derives from Biblical rather than Greek sources. Here we encounter the radical concept of human freedom, a democracy of understanding, and an instruction in the form of law that reflects the anxious concerns of human beings born of flesh and blood. A defense against irrational contact with the sacred is established in the Biblical world permitting the origin of just relations within a pluralistic humane society.

Unlike Socrates, Moses, the statesman, prophet, and law giver of ancient Israel, is linked to others by his own imperfection. He does not reach the land of promise, but glimpses it from a distant hill. The promise of existence must be accomplished by embodied human beings fatigued by the happenings of daily life. Eternity is not won in an instant but with the unfolding of a time for everything under heaven.

Our approach to the reading of the seminal texts of the West involves an attempt to understand these works accurately in their own context, but even more crucial is our desire to encounter these works as contemporary with ourselves and formative of our world. It is in this sense that we take up Nietzsche's challenge, presented in the opening of *The Genealogy of Morals*, that our first obligation to inquiry is that we knowers become known to ourselves.

A true humanistic education can only take place when the individual is able to develop his capacity for *logos* that derives from the patterns of knowledge and culture established in the Greek tradition that extends from Homer to Aristotle. But that education can only be realized by the person if existence is challenged by the immediacy and promise of human development enunciated in the Biblical tradition of the West. Only when knowledge and existence are both directly addressed and encountered can we say that we or our students are truly claimed by the humanities.

# *INDEX*

# Index

# A Note on the Authors

R. THOMAS SIMONE teaches in the Department of English at the University of Vermont, where he is the Director of the Integrated Humanities Program. He is the author of *Shakespeare and 'Lucrece': The Poem and the Plays* (Salzburg, 1975) and articles on modern drama. He is currently working on a study of the plays of Henrik Ibsen.

RICHARD I. SUGARMAN teaches in the Department of Religion at the University of Vermont. He served as Carneigie Teaching Fellow in Philosophy at Yale University. He is the author of *Rancor Against Time: The Phenomenology of Ressentiment* (Felix Meiner, 1980). He is currently working on a book on the philosophy of Emmauel Levinas.

ROBERT J. ANDERSON (contributing author) teaches in the Department of Philosophy at Washington College, Chestertown, Maryland. He received the Jacob Cooper Prize in Classical Philosophy at Yale University. He is completing a work on Plato's *Theatetus*.